Being H
to G

Simon Barrow, James Crossley, Elaine Graham,
Richard Holloway, Martyn Percy

Five talks given at a PCN Britain/Modern Church
conference in November 2013

St Marks CRC Press Sheffield

Together in Hope
Resources for Christian Faith Today

This series of resource books is the fruit of a number of organisations working together to give encouragement and hope to those who seek a credible Christian faith for the twenty first century.

We hope that these books will be helpful to those individuals and groups, inside and outside of the Church, who are exploring matters of faith and belief.

We are grateful to our authors and encourage others to offer their services.

For further information about the sponsoring organisations please see the back cover. If you wish to contact the editorial group email togetherinhope@googlemail.com

The current convenor is Adrian Alker

The books in this series can be bought via the PCN Britain and Modern Church websites (see back cover) or telephone 0845 345 1909.

Printed on recycled paper by Pickards.org.uk Sheffield (0114 275 7222)

The Contributors

Simon Barrow has been co-director of the religion and society think-tank Ekklesia since July 2005. A writer, theologian, commentator, consultant, adult educator, researcher and journalist, he contributes regularly to a wide variety of journals. From 2000-2005 Simon was global mission secretary for Churches Together in Britain and Ireland, which he also served as assistant general secretary until 2003. He was formerly adviser in education and training for the Anglican Diocese of Southwark (1991-1996) and has worked in current affairs journalism, theological education, development studies, and as the convenor of a national network of Christian social action groups. Simon has edited and co-edited a number of books, including *Consuming Passion: Why the Killing of Jesus Really Matters* (DLT: 2005), *Fear or Freedom? Why a warring church must change* (Shoving Leopard 2008). Simon Barrow's regular blog is FaithInSociety and his home page is: www.simonbarrow.net/

James Crossley is Professor of Bible, Culture and Politics at the University of Sheffield. He has a particular interest in the role of religion as a human phenomenon and its relationship to social, economic and ideological contexts, especially, but not exclusively, how this relates to the critical study of the origins, use and influence of New Testament texts. His books include *Jesus in an Age of Terror: Scholarly Projects for a New American Century* (Acumen Publishing 2008), *Reading the New Testament: Contemporary Approaches* (Routledge 2010), *Jesus in an Age of Neoliberalism: Scholarship, Intellectuals and Ideology* (Equinox: London and Oakville, 2012) He blogs at www.sheffieldbiblicalstudies.wordpress.com

Elaine Graham is Grosvenor Research Professor of Practical Theology at the University of Chester. Of herself, Graham writes: 'as a practical theologian, I am interested in the relationship between beliefs and actions, and whether religious commitment really makes a difference in today's world. In my teaching and research, I try to encourage people to connect the values of faith to a critical engagement with the dilemmas of everyday life.'

Her recent books include *Between a Rock and a Hard Place: Public Theology in a Post-Secular Age* (London: SCM Press, 2013), with Stephen R. Lowe, *What Makes a Good City? Public Theology and the Urban Church* (London: Darton, Longman and Todd, 2009).

She was the President of the International Academy of Practical Theology from 2005 to 2007 and was a member of the Archbishops' Commission on Urban Life and Faith, which published the report *Faithful Cities: A call for celebration, vision and justice* (Methodist Publishing House, 2006). She is also a member of the BBC Standing Conference on Religion and Belief, an occasional broadcaster and a contributor to the Church Times newspaper.

Richard Holloway was Bishop of Edinburgh from 1986 and was elected Primus of the Scottish Episcopal Church in 1992. He resigned from these positions in 2000. A Fellow of the Royal Society of Edinburgh, Holloway was Professor of Divinity at Gresham College in the City of London and is a former chair of the Scottish Arts Council. He has been a reviewer and writer for the broadsheet press for several years and is also a frequent presenter on radio and television, having hosted the BBC television series *When I Get to Heaven, Holloway's Road* and *The Sword and the Cross*. He is the author of many books, including more recently *Godless Morality: Keeping Religion out of Ethics* (1999), *Doubts and Loves: What is Left of Christianity* (2001), *On Forgiveness: How can we Forgive the Unforgivable?* (2002), *Looking in the Distance: The Human Search for Meaning* (2004), *How To Read The Bible* (2006), *Between the Monster and the Saint* (2008) and an autobiography, *Leaving Alexandria: A Memoir of Faith and Doubt* (2012).

Martyn Percy is Principal of Ripon College, Cuddesdon, Oxford. He is also Honorary Professor of Theological Education at King's College London, and Professorial Research Fellow at Heythrop College, University of London. His academic writing and research has mostly centred on the study of Christianity in contemporary culture, with interests spanning Anglicanism, theological education and modern ecclesiology. His publications include *Clergy: The Origin of Species* (Continuum 2006), and a trilogy focussing on ecclesiology with Ashgate Publishing - *Engaging Contemporary Culture: Christianity and the Concrete Church* (2005), *Shaping the Church: The Promise of Implicit Theology* (2010) and *The Ecclesial Canopy: Faith, Hope, Charity* (2012). The books *Anglicanism: Confidence, Commitment and Communion* (Ashgate, 2013) and *Thirty-Nine New Articles: An Anglican Landscape of Faith* (Canterbury Press, 2013) reflect this growing focus in his work.

Adrian Alker is Director of Mission Resourcing in the Diocese of West Yorkshire and the Dales. He was previously Vicar of St Marks Broomhill Sheffield, where he founded the Centre for Radical Christianity (St Mark's CRC). He is a trustee of PCN Britain and convenes the editorial group of the Together in Hope publications. He is author of *Christmas: Ancient Meanings, Modern Faith* (Together in Hope series).

Introduction

Revd Adrian Alker

When the book 'Honest to God' was first published in 1963 I was in the third year of my grammar school education, with little time at the age of 14 for religious debate. Rather my studies ranged from Latin through German to the seemingly endless and boring periods of Physics, whilst my emotional attention was on a young girl in my class called Sylvia.

And yet I was not unaware of the Church of England since I regularly turned up at Morning Prayer, having been confirmed alongside most youngsters in my class. Even in the heady days of the 1960's churchgoing in my particular part of Lancashire was very much still de rigeur. Only later, at university in the late 60's and at theological college in the later 70's, did controversy in matters of Christian thought and church practice become much more part of my experience and formation.

Whether you were at school in 1963, 1943 or 1993, the issues raised in Honest to God were then and are now, central to how we understand and experience the Christian faith and the church in every generation. As a serving bishop in the Church of England, John Robinson dared to ask the big questions which ordinary churchgoers may have asked themselves but which had rarely been voiced beyond the academy. Robinson asked his readers about their image of God. Was God an old man in the sky? That had to go. We were presented with the challenging model of 'depth' and 'ground of being' as previously developed by the German theologian Paul Tillich. We were offered in Jesus a 'Man for Others', a reorientation away from a focus on the God-Man who performs miracles and to see what a human being fully alive in God might be like. Since 1963, this quest for the 'real' Jesus has continued with increasing vigour. But what then are the implications of this rethinking for the conventions of prayer and worship? And if God is to be revealed primarily in the love and compassion of Jesus rather than in the prescriptions of God's Law, what does this say to our grasp of morality, of ethics?

Perhaps like many readers of this short book, I was and still am a pretty restless religious seeker. Even as a clergyman I have found it hard to swallow so much of the doctrinal and ecclesiastical structures which support and surround the Christian faith. I am by no means alone. 'Modern Church' began life as the Modern Churchman's Union in 1898, determined to take seriously the fruits of biblical scholarship, the findings of science and technology, the application of reason in the understanding of God. More recently the Progressive Christianity Network (PCN Britain) formed itself out of the progressive movement of theological thought in the USA. The leadership and membership of these two organisations decided to mark the fiftieth anniversary of the publication of 'Honest to God' by inviting five distinguished thinkers to speak around the themes in Robinson's book. Here we reproduce those five talks, together with questions at the close of each chapter, for you the reader or a group of readers meeting together to discuss.

The Conference was never intended to dwell on the past, to see the 1960's as some kind of liberal interlude when the church might have 'come of age'. Rather our speakers and their talks reflect our contemporary situation in the UK at the beginning of this third millennium. By being honest about the present and learning from the past we might be better placed to face, as religious seekers, an unknown and uncertain future.

In the first talk Elaine Graham, who also acted as chair of the conference, sets the scene, the background of Robinson and his book 'Honest to God'. She explores the main threads of Robinson's argument, crystallized in his comment to the Sunday Mirror of April 1963, 'If Jesus Christ means anything, he means that God belongs to this world.' Graham goes on to frame the essence of Robinson's thinking within the context of today's changed cultural and religious landscape.

In responding to Jesus, 'the Man for Others', James Crossley has some sharp and revealing arguments to bring to the discussion about studies of the historical Jesus. Just as Robinson attempts to tease out for his readers the Bonhoeffer question, 'What is Christ for Us Today?', so Crossley pulls no punches in his critique of many Jesus scholars whose construction of Jesus, he claims, more honestly reveals the neo liberalism of contemporary capitalism. Crossley begins his talk by quoting a 'curious equation' of A. Badiou, that 'Jesus plus Paul equals Marx plus Lenin'!

In his talk, Martyn Percy draws upon his deep knowledge of the Church of England in particular to lay down challenges for the church and its leadership today. Percy draws out a distinction and difference between seeing the church as an institution and regarding it as an organisation. If thinking about the latter leads to an over- emphasis on growth and management speak, on administrative and managerial processes, where will we be able to discover that talk about, and experience of, the God revealed in the Man for Others, of which Robinson spoke and which excited the faithful hearts of churchgoers in his day?

Simon Barrow has a long experience of contextualizing Christian faith in the light of contemporary social, economic and political thinking and raising questions of personal and corporate ethics thereby. In his talk, Barrow asks us to look more reflectively into our own hearts and minds to discover indeed those truths that might set us free but which might also be too much to bear. In attending to the church as an institution which might be a truth bearer, Barrow looks to George MacLeod, the founder of the Iona Community to wonder how local congregations can be reshaped into communities of transformation, touching upon Robinson's hope that the Church might always be subjected to the judgement of the Kingdom.

Finally in a gloriously enjoyed after-dinner talk (unscripted), Richard Holloway brought us back to think about God in his own erudite and radically honest way. In telling the story of a woman refusing a gay couple a bed in her lodgings, Holloway expresses respect and even affection for those who are faithful to a tradition which can nevertheless render people cruel. The cruelty stems from that type of faith which refuses to face up to the honest truth that the history of God, the very idea of God is one of constant flux and change. In some ways Richard Holloway, like John Robinson before him and others such as Jack Spong and David Jenkins represent those who have been appointed to high office in the Church and have kept alive the spirit of critical thinking and honest enquiry. Therein are grounds for hope!

One thing more needs to be said about how this conference and indeed this book came to be. Both the conference and the Together in Hope series are products of collaboration between organisations committed to open and exploratory thinking about Christian faith. Such organisations point to a future where there can be honest discussion and debate about matters of faith and belief. For those of us who are still 'on the inside' of the church, I can only suspect that such collaborative endeavour would have pleased Robinson. Let him have the last word:

'For the true radical is not the man (sic) who wants to root out the tares from the wheat so as to make the Church perfect: it is only too easy on these lines to reform the Church into a walled garden. The true radical is the man who continually subjects the Church to the judgement of the Kingdom, to the claims of God in the increasingly non-religious world which the Church exists to serve.' (p.140 Honest to God, SCM Press, 1963).

Being Honest...

Professor Elaine Graham

If we made a list of all the things we didn't have in 1963, such as mobile phones, the Internet and women priests, it would only serve to highlight the distance between our world and that of John A.T. Robinson. But the purpose of this conference is not to engage in some form of liberal 'ancestor worship', or even to indulge in reminiscences about what we were doing or even reading 50 years ago.

No: we certainly want to mark the anniversary, and celebrate the book's achievements, but more importantly, we should consider whether *Honest to God* still speaks to us, and how it might still be relevant today, and in what ways. What lay behind the core arguments of this book? What was it trying to achieve – and what did it actually manage to do in terms of long-term impact? Undoubtedly it inspired many people and generated much fierce debate. But what lessons can we learn; what encouragement can we draw; and what resources can we take for our own continuing journeys through life?

In this introduction, I want to remind us of some of the circumstances that gave rise to the publication of *Honest to God*, and sketch out some of its main arguments. But in keeping with attempts to bridge that gulf of time, we must ask how Robinson speaks to us now - even allowing for half a century of cultural, economic and religious change? In that spirit, I want to focus in particular on the idea of "honesty": to ourselves; to our context today; to the journey of faith; to our world.

Background

John A.T. Robinson (1917-83), was Dean of Clare College Cambridge (teaching New Testament) in the 1950's, Bishop of Woolwich 1959-69 and Dean of Chapel, Trinity College Cambridge. So he was an academic as well as a bishop. Before *Honest to God* he already had something of a reputation for speaking out on contemporary issues and the future of the Church. In 1960 he chaired a conference about the future of ordained ministry in which he challenged the elitism of the clergy and the exclusion of women from the priesthood (James, p. 80). In the Church Assembly (the precursor of General Synod), he spoke against capital punishment and, critically again, about the obstacles facing women training for lay ministry in the Church. He also became something of a celebrity for giving evidence for the defence in the notorious prosecution for obscenity against Penguin books in 1960 for the publication of *Lady Chatterley's Lover*, in which he defended the book's depiction of the essentially spiritual nature of the relationship, arguing that Christians should read the book for what it was saying about the value and sacredness of sexuality. So prior to the publication of *Honest to God* Robinson already had something of a reputation as a progressive, and of urging the Church to engage constructively not defensively with the modern world.

Honest to God had its genesis during a period of enforced rest for back problems, during which Robinson's wife Ruth read him Paul Tillich's *Shaking of the Foundations*. Tillich was a German theologian who had fled the Nazis in the 1930's and gone to teach in New York. His ideas were influential upon Robinson. It was that, and as Eric James his biographer argues, the experience of being a bishop in south London and witnessing 'the all but total alienation of the urban working class from the institutional church'.[1] So this is not just an academic, but as a church leader – a pastor and a Bishop - ministering at a time of significant social and cultural change, concerned that the Church should respond to these changing times.

And Robinson began to develop the idea of the need for a 'New Reformation' – in the Church's structures, its liturgies, its language, its core concepts – in order to be more accessible and relevant to an increasingly secular public. But for him, this Reformation didn't begin with, say, liturgical reform or a campaign for the ordination of women or programmes of reordering of church buildings – all of which were beginning to take place at this time. He decided to focus on the very nature and doctrine of God. That's maybe the first question for us: what's the relationship between an agenda of social reform, or cultural relevance, and the way the Church talks and thinks about God? For Robinson, the answer lay in his understanding of what it meant to be a 'radical':

> 'The reformist overhauls the institution and titivates the orthodoxy; and in this way everything is enabled to go on smoothly, and the revolution is averted. [For the revolutionary, on the other hand] the institution is rotten, the orthodoxy stinks and enslaves. The entire structure must be changed if man is to be free ... The radical must be a man of roots. The revolutionary may be déraciné, (torn from his roots) but not the radical. And that is partly why

[1] Eric James, *A Life of Bishop John A.T. Robinson: Scholar, Pastor, Prophet* (London: Collins, 1987), p. 111.

in our rootless world there are so few genuine radicals. Reformism, too, requires of necessity no depth of root, merely a feel for tradition: hence it can continue to flourish where men have lost their integrity. If the Establishment can thereby be preserved, it may be expedient that one man should die for the people. For man, after all, is made for the Sabbath. The roots of the radical, moreover, must go deep enough to provide the security from which to question, even to the fundamentals. No one can be a radical who is uncertain of his tenure – intellectually, morally, or culturally. Only the man who knows he cannot lose what the Sabbath stands for can afford to criticize it radically. Faith alone can dare to doubt – to the depths.[2]

So the radical goes to the roots, to the foundations of a thing. And for Robinson, that could be nothing other, nothing less, than the identity of God, since for him, God was the ground, the source, the essence of all reality. It is God, he believed, that gave meaning and direction to life: so if the Church was to recover its relevance, it had to address people at that very fundamental level, of what matters most. And that certainly meant imagining God and speaking about God in ways that spoke to contemporary experience and reconnected with people at large.

That meant doing away with redundant or anachronistic imagery which might once have worked for earlier generations, but which no longer conveyed anything meaningful. But he was astounded and quite wounded that his critics accused him of abandoning orthodox faith; for he saw himself as trying to reclaim it, rejuvenate it, even if it meant finding new concepts and language in order to do so.

In March 1963, in advance of the publication of *Honest to God*, *The Observer* published a preview of the book in which Robinson summarised his argument. The headline was 'Our Image of God must Go', which was not his but the paper's. But that maybe coloured the debate, in that it was perceived as a jettisoning of theism entirely (the very notion of any *kind* of God altogether) rather than, as Robinson saw it, an attempt to retrieve orthodoxy from layers of misinterpretation.

The book was a sensation: the first edition sold out on the day of publication.

---

[2] John Robinson, 'On Being a Radical', *The Listener* 21 February 1963, quoted in James, p. 113. Another thing that has changed in the past 50 years is the use of inclusive language!

So what were the main threads of Robinson's argument?

Chiefly, that God seemed disconnected from everyday life, and was only experienced at the margins or extremes. God was seen as remote, and dispassionate: someone - as he put it memorably, 'who exists somewhere out beyond the world – like a rich aunt in Australia – who started it all going, periodically intervenes in its running, and generally gives evidence of his benevolent interest in it.'[3] But as Robinson argued – in an article in the *Sunday Mirror* in April 1963, 'If Jesus Christ means anything, he means that God belongs to this world.'[4]

Let's explore those two points in more detail, then:

1. God, the Ground of Being

Images of God as isolated in heaven, the 'Old Man in the Sky', were for Robinson the things that 'had to go'. He characterized this as a 'supernaturalist' view of God, 'out there, above and beyond this world, existing in his own right alongside and over against his creation'.[5]   Instead, he favours a 'naturalist' model, as one that identifies God with 'what gives meaning and direction to nature'. Ways of speaking about God not as 'up there or out there' (Chap 1) but 'in here' – using language of depth, presence, interiority, intimacy even – speak far more profoundly of the reality of God. He used Paul Tillich's concept of God as 'Ground of our Being' to develop this:

> The name of this infinite and inexhaustible depth and ground of all being is <u>God</u>. That depth is what the word <u>God</u> means. And if that word has not much meaning for you, translate it, and speak of the depths of your life, of the source of your being, of your ultimate concern, of what you take seriously without any reservation. Perhaps, in order to do so, you must forget everything traditional that you have learned about God, perhaps even that word itself. For if you know that God means depth, you know much about him. You cannot then call yourself an atheist or unbeliever. For you cannot think or say: Life has no depth! Life is shallow. Being itself is surface only. If not. He who knows about depth knows about God.[6]

This is the total antithesis of any notion of a supernatural Being who exists apart from the world and who intervenes 'from

[3] J.A.T. Robinson, *Honest to God* (London: SCM Press, 1963), p. 30.
[4] Robinson, 'Why I Wrote It', *Sunday Mirror* (7 April 1963), quoted in James, p. 116.
[5] Robinson, *Honest*, p. 30.
[6] Paul Tillich, *The Shaking of the Foundations*, 1949, p. 63, quoted in Robinson, *Honest*, p.22.

without'.[7] In fact, 'God' according to this is not a Being at all, in the sense of a separate entity. Rather, God is 'the ultimate depth of all our being, the creative ground and meaning of all our existence'.[8]

This requires us to jettison everything we thought we knew. It even redraws the boundary between those who 'believe' and 'do not believe' in God. It is no longer whether we subscribe to the view of the Being outside ourselves, whose existence can be 'proved' logically and philosophically. It is, as Robinson begins to describe it, much more a question of what you are prepared to open yourself out to: not a cognitive or intellectual assent, so much as a willingness to encounter 'the unconditional ... the eternal.'[9]

But Robinson still looks to the God of the Bible, and considers Psalm 139 as an expression of God not as something over and above or beyond the everyday, but present and transforming the very deepest and most intimate parts of our being. Here, I think we can see his radicalism expressed in a desire to return to the (Biblical) roots of faith, to retrieve them from later misinterpretation, by articulating old concepts in new language.

I have been considering Robinson's idea of 'radicalism' as founded on his concepts of God, as necessarily beginning with the way we conceive of God. This implies that the way we live is indivisible from our fundamental images and understandings of God, the cosmos, our very world-view.

If God is no longer 'in the sky', however, there is still a sense that Robinson conceives of God as 'transcendent': but not in contrast with material things or embodied experience or human life - but anything that is superficial or reductionist or self-centred.

'Our contention has been that God is to be met not by a 'religious' turning away from the world but in unconditional concern for 'the other' *seen through to its ultimate depths*, that God is ... the 'personal ground of all that we experience'.

'... the way to 'the Father' – to acknowledgement of the 'ultimacy' of pure personal relationship - is thus only 'by the Son' – through the love of him in whom the human is completely open to the divine ...'[10]

2. Jesus, Man for Others

The centrality of Jesus as the One who reveals God most truly to us: as the Man for Others, as the embodiment of love – meaning

[7] *Honest*, p. 47.
[8] Ibid.
[9] *Honest*, p. 48.
[10] *Honest*, p. 63.

unconditional acceptance and forgiveness. 'This is precisely what we see Jesus doing in the Gospels', says Robinson in the *Sunday Mirror*, 'making and re-making men's lives, bringing meaning back to them.'[11]

We have to outgrow our dependency on the Father-God of tradition, the powerful but somewhat distant cosmic figure of the skies in order to rediscover Jesus, revealed in the frailty of human form, powerlessness and suffering. We find God in a human life fully lived as an expression of selfless love rather than by looking into the skies.

Here he draws on the theology of Rudolph Bultmann, another New Testament scholar, who took what he called a 'demythologising' view of Scripture, seeing much of the portrayal of Jesus there as reflecting a view of the cosmos, of miracles and the resurrection as an honest but time-bound attempt 'to express the real depth, dimension and significance of the *historical* (in italics) event of Jesus Christ.'[12] He also quotes Dietrich Bonhoeffer's appreciation of Bultmann, in saying that today we have to see God and Jesus in a 'non-religious' way.

I'm particularly struck by Robinson's suggestion that Jesus' most decisive revelation of God comes in his death and resurrection. This is where the unconditional love of God is disclosed: in Jesus' self-emptying and submission to the purposes of God. But this is not a surrender of omnipotent, heavenly power but of (human) self-centredness, of everything that stops short of the depths of Being. So one might even say that what Jesus surrenders is not his 'divinity' but his humanity – his part in the fallenness of the human condition – in order fully to recover the unconditional love in whose image we all have truly been created.

Jesus, then, is 'the Man for Others': the one who is totally open to the reality of God. In abandoning his own self-centredness, he opens himself to the reality beyond the mundane. And this is the way Jesus reveals God, says Robinson. He is not bound by worldliness and fear but by the liberating power of love. That is what opens him up totally to live in the reality of God.[13]

3. Worldly Holiness

But if Robinson is urging people to embrace this 'religionless Christianity', what is the place of the conventional marks of religion such as worship and prayer? This forms the basis of

[11] 'Why I Wrote It', quoted in James, *A Life*, p. 117.
[12] *Honest*, p. 34.
[13] *Honest*, p. 72-73.

Chapter 5 and is our third theme. But what he's arguing here is that these are not expressions of some holy world set apart, 'concerned essentially with the holy rather than the common, with 'religion' rather than 'life'. These only belong to, and indeed virtually constitute, that area or department of experience which appeals to 'the religious type', to those who 'like that sort of thing' or 'get something out of it'.'[14] Where we need to begin, says Robinson, is with a sacramental understanding of religion: of the holy in the midst of things, as that which sees the ordinary as revealing, not concealing or distracting from, the sacred. In the Eucharist (Robinson calls it Holy Communion), Christ reveals himself in the sharing of bread and wine. The holy places are outside the sanctuaries, beyond the enclaves of the pious, in the world of the common.

'The purpose of worship', he says then, 'is not to retire from the secular into the department of the religious ... but to open oneself to the meeting of the Christ in the common ...'[15]

Prayer, similarly, is not a retreat into an enforced separation from life, but an 'openness to the ground of our being'.[16]

4. The New Morality

Fourthly, there are consequences of this kind of radical God-talk for morality and the conduct of life. Robinson says that 'prayer and ethics are simply the inside and outside of the same thing.' [17] To rethink God as Love, as 'the ultimate ground and meaning of personal relationships'[18] is inevitably going to have practical effect – so again, thinking differently, conceiving of God radically, honestly, is not just an intellectual exercise but a profoundly ethical and practical pursuit.

The supernaturalist view tends to see God as the ultimate Law-giver who has sanctioned clear standards of right and wrong, which are unchangeable. Robinson invites us to see the dangers of a kind of rigid legalism – and he draws on the work of the ethicist Joseph Fletcher, who was later to write a book called *Situation Ethics*, which argued this at greater length. Love not law becomes the arbiter; not an absence of morality, but a 'new morality' (the title of Chapter 6) as 'the calculation of what is truly the most loving thing in this situation for every person involved.'[19]

[14] *Honest*, p. 85.
[15] p. 87.
[16] p. 102
[17] p. 105.
[18] Ibid.
[19] p. 119.

And what of this for the Church, as Robinson admits, the bastion of all that is most alienating about 'organized religion'? Interestingly, Robinson is not advocating the abolition of the Church. Indeed, something I think that has been missed but is still relevant, is his notion right in the closing pages that Christians need to belong to a collective body that cultivates a distinctive life-style which enables ordinary members to be fully rooted in the ways of Christ. This is close to what we would recognize in contemporary theology as a kind of 'virtue ethics'. But it's definitely a 'worldly' spirituality, and one that privileges the laity as the authentic expression of Christian service in the world – don't forget, in the Roman Catholic world, the second Vatican council is (1962-65) underway, and the idea of the Church in the world, embracing the worldliness of the world as signs of the Kingdom, are current at this time. And in a way we can hear Robinson favouring Establishment of the Church of England when he says, 'Anything that helps to keep its frontiers open to the world as Church of the nation should be strengthened and reformed'.[20] The Church is not 'a walled garden' for its own members, but seeks to subject itself 'to the claims of God in the increasingly non-religious world which the Church exists to serve.'[21]

Now, Robinson himself admits that these ideas are quite commonplace in theological circles but they hadn't percolated down to ordinary people. That's part of what he sees himself doing, not least because in his experience when he tried to teach Tillich and Bultmann and Bonhoeffer to ordinary people, they got quite excited.[22] But he realizes he's turning many established ideas upside down: it is, he says, like a Copernican revolution (the earth revolves around the sun not the other way around). In many respects, it's a 'reluctant revolution': 'Yet', he says:

> 'I feel impelled to the point where I can do no other. I do not pretend to know the answers in advance. It is much more a matter of sensing certain things on the pulses, of groping forward, almost of being pushed from behind. All I can do is to try to be honest – honest to God and about God – and to follow the argument wherever it leads.'[23]

What of today's context? Fundamentally, we live in a changed cultural and religious landscape, one quite different from that of 1963. What new challenges do our times represent?

---

[20] *Honest*, p. 139.
[21] p.140.
[22] *Honest*, p. 25
[23] p. 28.

A post-Christian, post-secular society[24]

Trends in some countries, especially in Western Europe, suggest two, unprecedented trends: increasing religious pluralism, coupled with a growing divide between those who identify as 'religious' and those who do not. The results of the 2011 Census in England and Wales indicate a continuing drift away from Christianity and an increase in religious disaffiliation. The census asked people to choose a religious identity, although the question[25] was voluntary. Results showed that whilst Christianity was still the largest religion, with 33.2 million people, or 59.3 per cent of the population, this had fallen from 71.7 per cent in 2001. The second largest religious group was Muslims, whose numbers grew from to 1.5 million to 2.7 million people (3.0 per cent to 4.8 per cent).

Significantly, there was a marked increase in those reporting no religion (from 14.8 per cent to 25.1 per cent). Whilst the Census question gave no insight into religious attitudes or into opinions about the public role of religion, other polls do offer further information in this respect. A poll conducted by *YouGov* in 2011 recorded that 40 per cent of adults interviewed professed no religion, 55 per cent were Christian and 5 per cent of other faiths. Age made a major difference, with only 38 per cent of the 18–34s being Christian and 53 per cent having no religion; whereas for the over-55s the figures were 70 per cent (Christian) and 26 per cent (no religion) respectively. 11 per cent of respondents claimed to attend a religious service once a month or more, 27 per cent less often, and 59 per cent never. Non-attendance was higher among the young (62 per cent for the 18–34s) than the old (54 per cent for the over-55s); higher among manual workers (62 per cent) than non-manuals (56 per cent) (YouGov 2011).

In November 2012, ComRes, on behalf of ITV News, conducted an online survey of 2,055 Britons aged 18 and over. 79 per cent agreed with the statement that religion is a cause of much misery and conflict in the world today; 11 per cent disagreed. 35 per cent agreed that religion is a force for good in the world, but 45 per cent disagreed, dissentients being more numerous among men (50 per cent) than women (41 per cent).

---

[24] Much of the next section is taken from Elaine Graham, *Between a Rock and a Hard Place: Public Theology in a Post-Secular Age* (London: SCM Press, 2013).
[25] 'What is your religion?'

All in all, these data point to a society in which religion is increasingly in retreat and nominal. With the principal exception of the older age groups, many of those who claim some religious allegiance fail to underpin it by a belief in God or to translate it into regular prayer or attendance at a place of worship. People in general are more inclined to see the negative than the positive aspects of religion, and they certainly want to keep it well out of the political arena. (ComRes 2012)

The religious landscape is more heterogeneous than ever before. The context into which Robinson spoke in *Honest To God* was already experiencing the impact of secularization, or the gradual decline of religious observance and diminishment of religion's prominence in society. These trends are still at work, in the secularist attitudes of Richard Dawkins and the New Atheism, with their intellectual scepticism, and a general distrust of religion having any influence upon politics, education, or law. Yet at the same time, there is a new visibility of religion and things spiritual: of interest in literature, film and popular culture as vehicles of the sacred; respect for the Archbishop of Canterbury's stance on debt and economic crisis; the way Pope Francis has caught the popular imagination as a potential reformer and man of the people.

Alongside this is greater attention to 'spirituality' rather than anything that might appear to be associated with formal, credal or institutional 'religion'. According to the author Robert Fuller, in his book of the same title, as many as 33 per cent of people in US identify as 'Spiritual but not Religious'. [26] Evidence suggests that this sentiment is, again, age-specific, with younger people less likely to identify with any kind of organized faith.

Fifty years after John Robinson, should this come as any surprise? One implication of what he had to say, arguably, was precisely to set people free from outmoded concepts and credal professions that had long since lost any power to speak meaningfully into their lives. Are we to lament, or celebrate, then, a greater openness to all sorts of diversity, a tolerance of heterodoxy, a relaxed attitude to 'belief' and greater emphasis on personal integrity and responsibility rather than social or moral conformity?

But of course alongside this liberalization we have the growth of fundamentalist religions – from the 1980s the re-emergence of conservative, mostly Republican-voting, evangelical Christianity. Despite the 1960s being a period of the end of colonialism by

[26] 2001.

European powers, and especially Great Britain, arguably, the past fifty years have seen new patterns of neo-colonialism – not only in economics and popular culture but in religion too, in the spread of that style of conservative, Bible-believing faith into the global south. Other forms of militant Islam, similarly, drown out more tolerant, reflective expressions of the faith. Religion remains a potent force: for nationalism, in movements attempting to resist globalization as well as being a force for greater globalization; for democratic and anti-democratic ends; as a source of human rights and emancipation; and as justification for the denial of rights to women and lesbian, gay, bisexual and transgender people.

So that suggests that rumours of the death of religion, or its transformation into a reasonable ethic of human progress, have been over-rated. We can't return to the securities of the past, or the certainties of Christendom; but equally, struggles for the very soul of religion, over the very question of who will win the right to claim that God is on their side, are still a real and pressing issue. The question of God, what images of God are evoked, and what is done in the name of God, are far from irrelevant. All the more reason, then, not to abandon the question of how to 'talk about God' but to pay renewed attention to the ways God-talk still shapes our world, for good and ill – and to ask ourselves what we can do about it.

Questions and Discussion Starters overleaf.

Questions and Discussion Starters

1. The beginnings of honesty, as in personal integrity and an authentic response to the needs of the world are rooted in the way we conceive of, talk about, behave towards, God. Think about this idea of 'radicalism' as beginning with concepts of God and the way we talk about God (which is what 'theology' means). How far do our views of the world, God, the cosmos, shape the way we live?

2. What does it mean to practise 'honesty' towards our beliefs – in God, Jesus, prayer, morality – today? Where is religion dishonest – or just in avoidance, especially in relation to most people's sense of what matters most to them?

3. Is it possible to be honest to one's intellect and experience and to the inherited sources of 'tradition'? How do we cultivate a spirituality, or habitus, of honesty?

4. What are the social and cultural challenges – and opportunities - facing us today in terms of talking about God in ways that will make a real difference? (What is the relationship between 'belief' or theology, and practice, ethics, action?)

Being Honest about Jesus

Professor James Crossley

1. Problems with Liberal and Radical Jewish Jesuses

While this essay will not be about John Robinson and his use of the then latest New Testament scholarship, it will be concerned with a certain kind of demythologising of the Gospel traditions, and even the historical Jesus himself. Let us begin with a curious equation, namely that Jesus plus Paul equals Marx plus Lenin:

> I am not the first to risk the comparison that makes of him [Paul] a Lenin for whom Christ will have been the equivocal Marx.'[27]

> Paul goes on to his true Leninist business, that of organizing the new party called the Christian community. Paul as a Leninist: was not Paul, like Lenin, the great 'institutionalizer,' and, as such, reviled by the partisans of 'original' Marxism-Christianity? Does not the Pauline temporality 'already, but not yet' also designate Lenin's situation in between two revolutions, between February and October 1917? Revolution is already behind us, the old regime is out, freedom is here – *but* the hard work still lies ahead.[28]

These claims may be unusual for traditional Jesus studies but they were made in some very prominent treatments of Paul by two of the most famous contemporary thinkers, Alain Badiou and Slavoj Žižek respectively. These readings of Christian origins are in no small part designed to challenge dominant postmodern or liberal understandings of Jesus and Paul. What I want to do is to likewise challenge the dominant liberal understandings of Jesus; or, alternatively, challenge people to be honest about the ideological dangers of seemingly benign historical reconstructions of Jesus.

As anachronistic as the statements by Badiou and Žižek may seem (and they would embrace this), we should hesitate should we wish to condemn them too quickly. Over the past 40 years, arguably the dominant rhetorical generalisation about the historical Jesus has been what has become a cliché: Jesus the Jew. This dominant scholarly construction has in fact been partly a product of postmodern and liberal forms of identity and dominant political

---

[27] A. Badiou, *Saint Paul: The Foundation of Universalism* (Stanford: Stanford University Press, 2003), p. 2.
[28] S. Žižek, *The Puppet and the Dwarf: The Perverse Core of Christianity* (Cambridge, Mass.: MIT Press, 2003), p. 9.

trends. For those unaware of recent scholarship on the ideological functions of contemporary Jesus scholarship, this may need spelling out and summarising in further detail.[29] If we leave aside Nazi scholarship for one moment, no contemporary scholar denies Jesus was Jewish. However, prior to the 1970s, mainstream scholarship typically argued that Jesus rejected much of what was believed to be central to Judaism. Jesus, it might typically have been argued, probably got rid of Sabbath laws and purity laws. Moreover, these Sabbath and purity laws deemed so central to Judaism were also deemed to be cold, harsh, and inadequate until Jesus came along and changed everything.

But something changed in the 1970s. Geza Vermes published his famous book, *Jesus the Jew*, in 1973 and saw Jesus as a figure firmly within Judaism and with Judaism was presented positively. Ever since Vermes' book, and particularly with the accompanying influence of E.P. Sanders,[30] most historical Jesus scholars will now bend over backwards to tell us how Jewish their Jesus is, with book titles regularly emphasising Jesus' Jewishness common enough – and all the while no one denying Jesus was Jewish! However, this dominant scholarly trend regularly constructs or assumes a construction of what constituted Jewish identity in the first century, before having their Jesus transcend this Jewish identity in some way, or at least presenting their Jesus as doing something new and unparalleled either generally or on some specific (and often crucial) issue, and typically involving the Torah and/or Temple. This, it should be added, is subtly different from Vermes' construction of Jesus the Jew because Vermes' Jesus was to do things that were effectively all paralleled in early Judaism. And so Vermes' challenge has been absorbed, domesticated and any overly problematic Otherness of this Jesus has been removed. Or as N.T. Wright put it about his Jesus: 'a very Jewish Jesus who was nevertheless opposed to some high-profile features of first-century Judaism'.[31]

---

[29] The following summary is based on the more extensive arguments (with a bibliography of influential scholarship) found in J.G. Crossley, *Jesus in an Age of Terror: Scholarly Projects for a New American Century* (London and Oakville: Equinox, 2008), pp. 143-194; J.G. Crossley, *Jesus in an Age of Neoliberalism: Quests, Scholarship and Ideology* (Sheffield: Equinox, 2012), pp. 105-132; 'A "Very Jewish" Jesus: Perpetuating the Myth of Superiority', *Journal for the Study of the Historical Jesus* 13 (2013), pp. 109-129; J.G. Crossley, *Jesus and the Chaos of History* (forthcoming), chapter 1, which includes a more expansive version of the ideas present here.

[30] E.g. E.P. Sanders, *Paul and Palestinian Judaism: A Comparison of Patterns of Religion* (London: SCM, 1977); E.P. Sanders, *Jesus and Judaism* (London: SCM, 1985).

[31] N.T. Wright, *Jesus and the Victory of God*, (London: SPCK, 1996), p. 93.

There are historical reasons for this soft superiority emphasis on a 'Jewish...but not *that* Jewish' Jesus. The 1967 Six Day War brought about major shifts in Anglo-American understandings of Israel and Judaism in popular, political, religious and intellectual culture, from indifference to a dominant discourse of staunch support, support which nevertheless has included attitudes of cultural and religious superiority in relation to Jews, Judaism and Israel. Thinking about the quest for the historical Jesus in such politicised and historicised ways shows how closely connected to dominant geo-political trends scholarship is. It further provides us with a way of understanding how the startling readings of Christian origins by Badiou and Žižek challenge the dominant postmodern Jesuses. We can go further still. Contemporary constructions of Jesus are intimately tied in with a dominant manifestation of capitalism we call neoliberalism which emphasises the power of the individual, image, free trade, private sector, freedom, and so on, the very economic model which has been facing such a crisis these past few years.[32] As Frederic Jameson and David Harvey in particular have shown, the connections between late capitalism/neoliberalism and the cultural 'condition' of postmodernity – with its emphasis on eclecticism, multiple identities, indeterminacy, depthlessness, and scepticism towards grand narratives – are clear enough. In this context, especially when we recall the 'liberal' in 'neoliberal', we might begin by thinking of the marketplace of multiple, sometimes competing, Jesuses (eschatological prophet, sage, Cynic-like social critic, wisdom teacher, Mediterranean Jewish peasant, or any combination of the types).

One key corollary of these intersecting trends in contemporary capitalism has been multiculturalism. A dominant liberal form of multiculturalism that has emerged over the past 40 years which embraces others but has to ensure that anything problematic is removed; or, in terms of a dominant discourse of contemporary liberal multiculturalism, the Other is welcomed but without the Otherness in this liberal democratic embrace. Popular statements on 'religion', or specific religious practices, highlight this point neatly. For instance, we might regularly hear of liberal phrases like 'true Islam' which is deemed to be spiritual and not violent. In this tradition, 'true Christianity' is also a religion of peace with the Crusades some kind of perversion and understanding Jesus as a peace-loving figure crucified for his message of love rather than

---

[32] For detailed discussion see Crossley, *Jesus in an Age of Neoliberalism*.
[33] See e.g. R.T. McCutcheon, *Religion and the Domestication of Dissent: or, How to live in a less than perfect nation* (London and Oakville: Equinox, 2005).

the man who called Gentiles 'dogs' and condemned people to Hades-fire. This ideological move to decide which is the 'true' manifestation attempts to make sure such people are, or are not, part of liberal discourses on 'religion'.[33] And this multicultural acceptance of the Other deprived of Otherness is precisely what we see with dominant views on Jesus the Jew: scholarship regularly embraces this 'very Jewish' Jesus but the stranger bits are now 'redundant', to use another phrase from Wright.[34] But is this not just a soft form of the old myth of superiority?

Collectively, the above is one reason why I would label almost all mainstream historical Jesuses as 'liberal', whether scholars like it or not. But what do we make of the numerous anti-imperial (and even anti-capitalist) Jesuses that have been common over the past forty years? Surely they would buck such trends! I am not entirely convinced that they do, even if we should not throw the baby out with the bathwater. For a start, the awkward relationship with the construction of Judaism remains strong: Judaism often still implicitly represents the oppressor and Jesus the oppressed.[35] Another reason why I am not convinced is that anti-capitalism is widespread and absorbed within neoliberal capitalism. As Žižek put it:

> Today, when everyone is 'anticapitalist,' up to the Hollywood 'socio-critical' conspiracy movies (from *The Enemy of the State* to *The Insider*) in which the enemy are the big corporations with their ruthless pursuit of profit, the signifier 'anticapitalism' has lost its subversive sting. What one should problematize is rather the self-evident opposite of this 'anticapitalism': the trust in the democratic substance of the honest Americans to break up the conspiracy.[36]

Žižek takes this argument in a different direction with reference to 'peasant' and 'revolutionary' contexts increasingly familiar to studies of the context of Jesus. In his review of the film *Avatar*, Žižek pointed out that at the same time as the film was generating one billion dollars in under three weeks, there was in fact something resembling its plot happening in the Indian state of Orissa. Here land was sold to mining companies which provoked an armed rebellion. Consequently, there were propaganda and military attacks from the Indian state and a vicious conflict ensued. Žižek added:

---

[34] Wright, *Victory*, pp. 399-402.
[35] A.-J. Levine, *The Misunderstood Jew: The Church and the Scandal of the Jewish Jesus* (San Francisco: HarperCollins, 2006).
[36] S. Žižek, 'Do We Still Live in a World?' http://www.lacan.com/zizrattlesnakeshake.html.

So where is Cameron's film here? Nowhere: in Orissa, there are no noble princesses waiting for white heroes to seduce them and help their people, just the Maoists organising the starving farmers. The film enables us to practise a typical ideological division: sympathising with the idealised aborigines while rejecting their actual struggle. The same people who enjoy the film and admire its aboriginal rebels would in all probability turn away in horror from the Naxalites, dismissing them as murderous terrorists. The true avatar is thus *Avatar* itself – the film substituting for reality.[37]

Putting the motivations, beliefs and practices of individual scholars to one side (I doubt any scholar is deliberately dishonest), it is difficult to see how contemporary historical Jesus scholarship as a field of study, or the popular trend of making the historical Jesus a socio-political radical, is having any significant political impact. That sounds blindingly obvious and it is – we never really expect it to! Perhaps we should be more honest about the function of some of our great heroes in the quest for the historical Jesus. Crossan and Borg may have Jesuses who are radical political figures but arguably their most significant ideological function, or indeed greatest success, is to sell books to liberal audiences on a large scale and Borg's mystical, Buddhist-esque Jesus effectively ends up looking internally, the ultimate capitalist subject.[38]

Strands of Liberation Theology provide an important point of comparison because here we have influential church organisations dedicated to liberation and a situation where there has been serious peasant exploitation and imperialism of the sort found in historical Jesus books and reconstructions of Jesus' context. Liberation theology *has* had an impact, hence the reason various figures in Latin America were beaten and murdered, something we might not expect to happen to Borg-inspired liberal American churches.[39] To paraphrase Mark Fisher's analysis of *Wall-E*, radical historical Jesuses perform our anti-capitalism and radicalism for us, allowing us to consume endless historical Jesus books with impunity.[40]

---

[37] S. Žižek, 'Return of the Natives', *New Statesman* (March 4, 2010), http://www.newstatesman.com/film/2010/03/avatar-reality-love-couple-sex

[38] E.g. M.J. Borg, *Conflict, Holiness, and Politics in the Teachings of Jesus* (orig.: Edwin Mellen: New York, 1984; Harrisburg, Pa: Trinity Press International, 1998); M.J. Borg, *Jesus, a New Vision: Spirit, Culture, and the Life of Discipleship* (London: SPCK, 1993).

[39] Cf. N. Chomsky, *Understanding Power* (New York: New Press, 2002), p. 154.

[40] M. Fisher, *Capitalist Realism: Is There No Alternative?* (Winchester, UK, and Washington, USA: Zero Books, 2009), p. 12: 'the film performs our anti-capitalism for us, allowing us to consume with impunity'.

And to this we might add: why do we need the historical Jesus to critique contemporary manifestations of power? And what if Jesus suggested things we find unpleasantly racist? And would we really agree with him if he thought that a theocracy would be imposed on the world imminently with the wrong people being punished terribly? It might even be said to be dishonest to suggest that such sentiments were absent from the Gospel tradition and so we need to find alternative ways of understanding the historical process and the structures of injustice in human societies incorporating any problematic Otherness this might entail and without so easily displacing our anti-capitalist fantasies into the long, distant past. There have, of course, been attempts to retrieve Jesus' Otherness by locating him in the context of the strange 'Mediterranean', often synonymous with the 'Arab World', but these too seem to me to be by-products of dominant Orientalist discourses over the past 40 years.[41] Let me give one explicit example from a book on Jesus and the Gospels by the leading social scientific critic of the New Testament, Bruce Malina. Malina has influentially argued that social models from the 'Mediterranean' shed light on the social world of Jesus. Among the many quotable passages where Malina makes generalisations about 'the Arab world' and 'the Mediterranean', the following (which apparently holds for 'village Mediterraneans' in general) is particularly notable, not least because it comes by way of Raphael Patai's long outdated book, *The Arab Mind*, a book, incidentally, used in Washington circles and was the intellectual underpinning of Abu Ghraib:

> ...personalization of problems goes so far in the Arab countries that even material, technical difficulties accompanying the adoption of elements of Western civilization are considered as resulting from human malevolence and felt to be a *humiliation*...Where the Arab encounters an obstacle he imagines that an enemy is hidden. Proud peoples with a weak 'ego structure' tend to interpret difficulties on their life path as personal humiliations and get entangled in *endless lawsuits* or throw themselves into the arms of *extremist political movements. A defeat in elections*, a risk that every politician must face in a democracy, appears to be such a humiliation that an Arab can thereby be induced without further ceremony to take up arms against the victor and the legal government... [italics original][42]

[41] Crossley, *Jesus in an Age of Terror*, pp. 59-142.
[42] R. Patai, *The Arab Mind* (revised edition; New York: Hatherleigh Press, 2002). The version used by Malina is quoted in B.J. Malina, *The Social World of Jesus and the Gospels* (London: Routledge, 1996), p. 63.

The political ramifications of these sorts of arguments do not need spelling out (and let us not forget that this comes from a book on the social world of Jesus and the Gospels). What is also significant about 'the Mediterranean'/'the Middle East' is not only that it is colonized by scholarship but also what kind of famous Jesuses it can produce. Portraits may differ wildly but the logic of superiority remains in important historical Jesus scholarship. Indeed, there are scholars who have systematically applied the backdrop of the Mediterranean to an understanding of the historical Jesus and none more so than John Dominic Crossan. But, despite making some significant advances, should we not apply some of that honesty again?

Crossan's Mediterranean Jewish peasant becomes arguably the most famous liberalized (in a widely recognized sense) Jesus of recent times, does it not? For all the anti-imperial rhetoric of Crossan it is noticeable that Crossan's Jesus stands over against the alien Mediterranean world. The world of honour and shame which supposedly characterises 'the Mediterranean' is, so the argument goes, profoundly challenged. And against this fixed Mediterranean world is a Jesus with common table fellowship, brokerless kingdom, subverting the system, playing around with gender categories, and so on. Crossan's Jesus is, in many ways, and certainly unintentionally, representative of liberal America, or perhaps the liberal West, overcoming the illiberal East.

Of course, it still remains that we have Jesuses, or studies of the early traditions, as well as significant elements of Crossan's work and work on Palestine in the first century, which really do point to ways in which to understand the chaos and upheaval of Jesus' time, not to mention the socio-economic structures which have contributed to injustice in human history.[43] This may provide a means to think about historical development without so obviously resorting to Jesus merely as an avatar for anti-capitalist fantasies. On one level we might reinforce the argument (legitimately, I would add) that the critique these Jesuses brings displaces critique safely to the past. But this is where the point about not throwing out the baby with the bathwater becomes significant. What such scholarship potentially shows is that Jesus, or the early Jesus tradition, should also be seen as a product of historical change and

---

[43] E.g. (among many) H. Moxnes, *The Economy of the Kingdom: Social Conflict and Economic Relations in Luke's Gospel* (Philadelphia: Fortress, 1988); K.C. Hanson and D.E. Oakman, *Palestine in the Time of Jesus: Social Structures and Social Conflicts* (Minneapolis: Augsburg Fortress, 1998); W.R. Herzog, *Prophet and Teacher: An Introduction to the Historical Jesus* (Louisville: WJK, 2005); D.A. Fiensy, *Jesus the Galilean: Soundings in a First Century Life* (Piscataway; Gorgias, 2007).

development. What I want to do is to shift the focus on to using Jesus as a means of understanding historical change and the ways in which power functions in human society, irrespective of whether his teaching is nice, terrible, weird, useful or seemingly irrelevant.

2. The Opium of the People?

Marx's famous saying that religion is 'the opium of the people' is often taken as an attack on religion. However, there is increasing awareness that to argue this is to rip the saying out of context; for Marx said fully: 'The wretchedness of religion is at once an expression of and protest against real wretchedness. Religion is the sigh of the oppressed creature, the heart of a heartless world, and the soul of soulless conditions. It is the *opium* of the people.'[44] There are problems if we take this to assume 'religion' in essentialist terms and so I will work with the assumption that those discourses we typically understand to be 'religious' are part of a competing network of discourses used by human beings to understand and negotiate the world.

With that said, we can acknowledge that the world of what we typically understand as 'religion' is not always as romantic as a more literal reading of the Marx passage might suggest but still accept that there is something in it in the sense that discourses we might find unusual or strange (or usual and familiar) can, of course, tell us something about material and historical change and structure. And it is an important counter to the overtly liberal New Atheism of Richard Dawkins, Sam Harris, Martin Amis, A.C. Grayling and others we have been experiencing over the past ten years. For Dawkins and others it is precisely the problematic (and essentialist) 'religion' that is at the heart of so many of the great ills in the world today, including September 11.

Not only does analysis of Dawkins show what is so problematic about assuming the mysterious 'religion' as a cause of violence, including what happened on September 11, but a counter reading shows how a (qualified) understanding of Marx is along the right lines for understanding historical change.[45] For instance, some of the standard reasons given for the rise of revolutionary Islam or 'fundamentalism' are a complex range of issues, including: the

---

[44] K. Marx, *A Contribution to the Critique of Hegel's 'Philosophy of Right'* (Cambridge: Cambridge University Press, 1970), p. 131.
[45] E.g. R. Dawkins, 'Religion's misguided missiles', *Guardian* (15 September 2001); M. Amis, 'The Voice of the Lonely Crowd', *Guardian* (1 June, 2002); S. Harris, *The End of Faith: Religion, Terror, and the Future of Reason* (London: Simon & Schuster, 2004); M. Amis, 'The age of horrorism', *Observer* (10 September, 2006); R. Dawkins, *The God Delusion* (London: Bantham, 2006).

decline of secular nationalism in North Africa and the Middle East; the specific context of the key American ally, Saudi Arabia, the homeland of the majority of the September 11 killers; the destructive sanctions on Iraq; Palestine; the petro-crash; the rise of slums and population growth; and US support for various dictators.[46] None of these factors are properly discussed among prominent New Atheists. Are they being honest? Presumably. Ignorance isn't dishonesty, after all. What we can say is that the ideological function of blaming 'religion', or even using 'religion' to justify torture in the case of Sam Harris, almost solely masks numerous uncomfortable material reasons for historical change.

What I want to argue then is that, with all cultural differences duly accepted, what we might understand to be 'religion' in the case of the historical Jesus, or indeed all other human discourses we might label entirely differently, can be as much a reaction to the heartless world as some of those more contemporary examples. In fact, in the case of a first century figure or the associated early tradition, we should probably accept one scholarly cliché: 'religion' (however understood) cannot really be separated from the rest of society. Or: understanding the historical Jesus can provide a way of thinking about Jesus as a useful means of understanding human society and history, rather than simply producing yet another Jesus portrait for the marketplace or producing another argument that Jesus was a Great Man who changed everything by the unique force of his will.

But then biography does not have to be the way of the typical historical Jesus book. Some historians have not been particularly impressed with a basic descriptive-biographical approach to history and historical Jesus scholars could have more fully embraced Marx's famous (and elsewhere widely accepted) pre-inclusive language saying: 'Men make their own history, but they do not make it just as they please; they do not make it under circumstances chosen by themselves, but under circumstances directly encountered, given and transmitted from the past.'[47]

For those more biographically inclined, there are similar possibilities raised in a defence of the biographical form as serious history by Ben Pimlott.[48] Pimlott was critical of the lengthy and meticulously researched descriptions of the lives of someone-or-other. Instead he emphasized that

---

[46] For a full discussion see Crossley, *Jesus in an Age of Terror*, pp. 58-99.
[47] K. Marx, *The Eighteenth Brumaire of Louis Bonaparte* (New York: International Publishers, 1963), p.15.
[48] B. Pimlott, 'Brushstrokes,' in M. Bostridge (ed.), *Lives for Sale: Biographers' Tales* (London & New York: Continuum, 2004), pp. 165-170.

...far from underplaying social factors, the good biographer highlights them, to give *added precision* to the story. Good biography is flexible, *making unexpected connections across periods of time and including unexpected essays on topics which, for the involvement of the subject, might never get written about at all'* [my italics].[49]

It follows that there should be nothing contradictory about writing about specific historical figures with a concern for explaining social change.[50] As we will see, socio-economic changes in Galilee as Jesus would have been growing up provide some important reasons for the emphases of the earliest Jesus tradition and why the Jesus movement emerged when and where it did.

3. Contextualizing a Life of Jesus

Wide-ranging socio-economic explanations of historical change are not common in New Testament scholarship. What we typically find in the major works of so-called New Testament Histories is a relentless description of ideas or how social context explains ideas. At best the explanatory force is too often akin to the surface level of events and historically inexplicable (as Braudel or Marx at least would have it) without the deeper movements of the social, geographical, economic etc.

So, how might we go about a wider explanation? We may begin with the 'why there and then?' that, of course, so interested Crossan in some of the most important aspects of his work.[51] The Jesus movement did not emerge out of the blue and here we can summarise some of the key points from the socio-historical work on first century Galilee which helps us understand why the movement emerged when and where it did. By the time Jesus' ministry was in full swing, Galilee had witnessed the building and re-building of the key urban centres, Tiberias and Sepphoris, with significant socio-economic consequences. Such urbanisation, which almost inevitably extracts resources from the countryside, is a key feature of the kinds of activity that underlie the rare events of peasant unrest and the emergence of millenarian or utopian groups in aristocratic or agrarian empires like Rome, calling for changes ranging from the reactionary to revolutionary.[52]

It is also linked in with the general socio-historical arguments: significant socio-economic change (perceived or otherwise) and

[49] Pimlott, 'Brushstrokes', pp. 169-70.
[50] Pimlott, 'Brushstrokes', p. 166.
[51] J.D. Crossan, *The Birth of Christianity. Discovering what happened in the years immediately after the execution of Jesus* (New York: HarperCollins; Edinburgh: T&T Clark, 1998).
[52] J.H. Kautsky, *The Politics of Aristocratic Empires* (Chapel Hill: University of North Carolina, 1982) e.g. pp. 278-303.

the dislocation of peasant land are major factors in peasant unrest and reaction, with help often (but not exclusively as certain Marxists would have it) coming from outside the peasantry.[53] The labour and materials had to come from somewhere and so people would have faced the possibility of dislocation (cf. *Ant.* 18.36-38). It is no coincidence that there was a full scale revolt against Rome in 66-70CE, accompanying which are reports of great hatred levelled at Sepphoris and Tiberias (*Life* 30, 39, 66-68, 99, 374-84), as well as a period that gave us figures such as Theudas and John the Baptist. It is in this context of social upheaval that we can contextualise the emergence of the Jesus movement and the earliest Palestinian traditions.

An important qualification is required here: *perception*. Unrest and social upheaval do not simply have to be a reaction to, or the result of, a decline in the general standard of living or a reaction to people being vigorously and explicitly exploited (though, of course, they may be). The way in which we might alternatively conceptualise conflict is to focus on whether the populace *perceive* change for the better (ask voters in the North and Home Counties if they think Thatcher boosted the standard of living and you will get different answers). In terms of the context of the earliest Palestinian tradition, the rebuilding of Sepphoris and the building of Tiberias, or, further south, the major extension of the Jerusalem Temple, we can at least suggest that the socio-economic situation would have been significantly changed and not everyone would have perceived changes in traditional lifestyle for the better, as the Gospel tradition may well attest. Why else do we get the millenarianism of the kingdom of God or the stark and continual emphases on rich people not passing through an eye of a needle, a rich man burning in Hades for no other reason than being rich, or serving either God or Mammon?

The emergence of millenarian or utopian groups in aristocratic or agrarian empires is crucial for making those unexpected connections across periods of time. A striking, albeit anachronistic, example is the English civil wars of the mid-seventeenth century. The most obvious reading here would be Christopher Hill's account of the civil wars as a bourgeois revolution paving the way for longer term capitalist development. As part of this 'revolution', Hill famously gave much attention to radical developments 'from below' involving figures such as Gerrard Winstanley and groups

---

[53] For discussions in biblical studies see e.g. Crossan, *The Birth of Christianity*, pp. 154-57; Herzog, *Prophet and Teacher* (with creative discussion of Paulo Freire); Crossley, *Why Christianity Happened*.

such as the Levellers, Quakers, and Diggers, all of which would have to be dealt with, tamed, ignored, and/or domesticated.[54]

This 'world turned upside down' provided a context for unheard of radical claims concerning democracy, sexuality, theology, God, education, millenarianism and so on, with millenarianism and related ideas providing a general perspective important for understanding Jesus and Christian origins.[55] Christopher Hill's work may have long gone out of fashion and his particular Marxist reading seriously challenged, but the general point that this 'world turned upside down' led to longer term changes, suppression and/or developments in science, theology, literature, politics, democracy, philosophy and so on, all to be taken up vigorously in the Enlightenment, remains an important one, as Michael Braddick has more recently argued.[56]

We might think of analogous contexts of chaotic social upheaval contributing to shifts in, and explosions of, ideas and thinking (whether revolutionary, reactionary, creative, culturally bizarre, peaceful, violent, accidental, and so on) which may have huge long-term impacts, being clamped down almost immediately, or have potential unrealised, from the French Revolution to the Spanish Civil War, from the Peasants' Revolt to the Iranian Revolution. But, with historical and cultural differences duly acknowledged, there is something of the logic about the emergence of (culturally) radical groups and ideas when we think of more ancient agrarian societies. And, of course, not only did early first century Galilee witness some significant socio-economic changes but also Palestine of the first century witnessed some monumental changes, culminating in the two famous revolts against Rome.

From this, to at least some degree, emerge Christianity and the consolidation of Judaism among the rabbis. These developments should not simply be restricted to the revolts themselves but were part of thinking that emerged from a series of significant cultural changes intersecting with specific cultural traditions already present in first century Palestine. Moreover, we also know, of course, that Christianity (and Judaism) would stretch beyond

---

[54] C. Hill, *The World Turned Upside Down: Radical Ideas during the English Revolution* (London: Temple Smith, 1972).

[55] See e.g. D.C. Allison, *Jesus of Nazareth: Millenarian Prophet* (Philadelphia: Fortress, 1998), 78-94 and D.C. Allison, *Constructing Jesus: Memory, Imagination, and History* (London: SPCK, 2010), pp. 85-88, who approaches the historical Jesus from the perspective of cross-cultural millenarian groups. Cf. C. Rowland, *Christian Origins: An Account of the Setting and Character of the Most Important Messianic Sect of Judaism* (London: SPCK, 1989), pp. 87-91, 111-117.

[56] M. Braddick, *God's Fury, England's Fire: a New History of the English Civil Wars* (London: Allen Lane, 2008), e.g. p. xxv.

Palestine and across the Empire and, in the case of Christianity, would become the Empire. A not-so-hypothetical forthcoming book might also look at some (and only some) of the ways in which broader and long term trends in the ancient world intersected with the tradition emerging from the upheaval in Palestine.

There are clear and important methodological echoes of work on genealogies here.[57] In this sense, historical analysis looks for the somewhat chaotic development of ideas without recourse to implied metaphysical origins. This qualification is especially important because the critique of the quest for origins obviously lies at the heart of the quest for the historical Jesus and could be mistaken for lying at the heart of an approach which looks at social upheaval and the redirection of ideas. However, a not-so-hypothetical forthcoming book on the historical Jesus, while hardly disavowing totalising history, does *not* have to be the search for the pure, essential origins of Christianity, as if at its heart lies the scholarly construct of the influential historical figure of Jesus. Instead, we are tracing and unravelling the details of the uneasy, accidental, purposeful, discontinuous, and implicit meanings in the developments of ideas as they appeared in particular times and places.

4. Reconstructing and Recontextualising Jesus Traditions

So far I have emphasised 'Jesus traditions' over the 'historical Jesus'. This requires not only an explanation but some more honesty that I am not sure scholars are always comfortable with, though I suspect more than a few would agree with what I am going to suggest, even if they would not always admit it publicly! The rhetoric of scholarship can get carried away with how much we can actually know about Jesus. The 'criteria of authenticity' for establishing the historical Jesus are deeply flawed. Multiple attestations of independent sources and forms never really got us back to the historical Jesus, they only got us back to early tradition. Miracles, after all, turn up across the Gospel tradition and this only shows that miracle stories were very popular from an early date, not, as some conservative scholars have tried to suggest, that we have anything approaching proof for the historicity of miracle stories. The criterion of embarrassment only told us, *if we were lucky*, that some writers were embarrassed by certain traditions

---

[57] M. Foucault, 'Nietzsche, Genealogy, History', in D.F. Bouchard (ed.), *Language, Counter-Memory, Practice: Selected Essays and Interviews* (Cornell University Press: Ithaca, 1977), pp. 139–64.

but, implicitly, that others were not. It too could only take us to early tradition...*at best*.

Even stories which appear to have a firm grounding in first century Palestinian culture are ultimately limited in understanding the historical Jesus.

We might take as an example Mark 2.23-28, the story of Jesus' disciples being criticised by Pharisees for plucking grain on the Sabbath. Plucking grain is not forbidden in biblical Law but its legality was debated, as the following example from the Mishnah shows:

'Six rules did the men of Jericho make...For three the Sages criticised them...[2] they eat on the Sabbath fruit which had fallen under a tree...' (m. *Pesahim* 4.8).

Furthermore, Josephus and other roughly contemporary evidence is clear that different groups bitterly disputed with one another over the correct interpretation of the Law so, again, it is certainly plausible that a dispute over plucking of grain could take place. In addition to echoing Jewish statements about human lordship over the Sabbath, Mark 2.27-28 is one of the prime examples of an Aramaism in the Gospels: 'The Sabbath was made for humankind, and not humankind for the Sabbath; so the Son of Man is lord even of the Sabbath.' The Greek (*ho huios tou anthropou*) was not a Greek idiom but reflects idiomatic Aramaic (some form of *bar nash*). The Aramaic idiom could be used to refer to the speaker as well as a wider group of people (perhaps akin to 'someone in my position', as one of the older suggestions claimed).[58] Mark 2.27-28, in other words, is in the form of parallelism and clearly reflects idiomatic Aramaic. To top things off, Luke and Matthew drop Mark's generalising 2.27 ('The Sabbath was made for humankind, and not humankind for the Sabbath') and make *The* Son of Man a title for Jesus and Jesus alone.

Collectively, we might make a case for this sort of passage going back to the historical Jesus. What is more, details of what can and cannot be done on the Sabbath do not seem to be high on the agenda, as far as we know, for the early church, where the issue is whether the Sabbath should be observed at all. We have similar traditions in the Gospels.

We have discussions over pure and impure which are about the role of washing hands or cups which make wide ranging assumptions about Jewish purity law. These sorts of debates are

---

[58] For full discussion see M. Casey, *The Solution to 'the Son of Man' Problem* (London and New York: T&T Clark, 2007).

about how to interpret biblical purity correctly and are seemingly of minimal interest to the early church. So, collectively, do not disputes such as plucking grain on the Sabbath or washing hands or cups reflect the historical Jesus? Possibly. They certainly look like they go back to early Palestinian tradition. *But that is as far as we can go*. We do not actually know if Jesus spoke the words or carried out the deeds attributed to him and, despite some scholarly confidence, we could not possibly know anyway. Clearly, there was some interest in the legal material in the Gospel tradition but that might further suggest that there might have been early Christians (or whatever they called themselves) who were interested in what can and cannot be done on the Sabbath so why could they not have invented or tampered with Jesus traditions? All we can ultimately do is work with generalisations about the early traditions and remain agnostic on ultimate historicity.

But the failure of the criteria – and even the strongest arguments in favour of historicity, is actually a blessing. This failure *should* get us away from the fiction that we found the great individual at the core and the lack of confidence about recovering the historical Jesus should *focus* attention more on the range of traditions which may have been part of the social upheaval of early-mid first century Palestine, as we saw with the millenarianism and sayings on rich and poor in the Gospel tradition.

So, for instance, the Sabbath or purity disputes tell us that there was an early concern for upholding biblical commandments concerning purity whilst simultaneously critiquing expansions of the law to all of everyday life. Disputes over purity law, particularly with Pharisees, were part of an identity reaction to perceived imperialism (directly or indirectly, cultural or brutal) going back to the Maccabean revolt. The Pharisees were a popular urban expression of Jewish identity (at least according to Josephus) and it seems Herod Antipas knew this when he built Tiberias on a graveyard, which allowed Antipas to populate the town with displaced Galileans and, through land gifts, the more aristocratic. By building it on a graveyard, the site of the worst sort of impurity (corpse impurity), he was, as has been suggested from time-to-time, presumably discouraging Pharisees from getting in the way.

Yet, there were clearly plenty of Galileans who did not care so much about the expansion of purity laws and we know that there was sufficient widespread indifference or disagreement with Pharisaic opinions and agreement with something like the position attributed to Jesus. It seems that the Jesus traditions come from such circles where a competing dedication to Jewish identity also emerged. It is probably noteworthy that the Jesus tradition calls the Pharisees 'hypocrites' (e.g. Mark 7; att. 23), or more precisely, 'actors', perhaps the sort that might be present in the theatre at Sepphoris.

But why does purity remain an issue in the Gospel tradition? Specifically Jewish purity law was not an issue for non-Jews and non-Jews could not transmit impurity. It is little surprise this theme turns up in the early church – it just was not an issue outside Palestine. Yes, this would strongly suggest that its presence in the Gospel tradition is due in part to what was happening in Palestine and so we are dealing with early Palestinian tradition. But why keep such material? One reason could simply be that a Gospel like Matthew had one eye on purity debates in its own context but it was more widespread than that.

What also happens in the purity passages is a major emphasis on correct behaviour or morality – what comes out of the heart is what defiles – and this emphasis on correct behaviour is precisely what we find in certain vice lists and other descriptions of what *Gentiles* are really like (e.g. they murder and blaspheme, they are idolaters, they will sleep with anyone or anything, and so on) and *that* is why they really are a problem. This is one explanation as to why the Gospels might retain such early purity tradition: to tell people how, or how not, to behave. Notice, for instance, that the major purity passage in Mark 7.1-23 ends with a vice list before Jesus moves into 'Gentile' territory and heals the daughter of the Syro-Phoenician woman. Purity traditions initially survived in part not as a point of contrast but because of their usefulness in stressing 'inner' morality. Over time, the survival of the language of purity would lead to its Christianisation or reinterpretation. The precise debates about purity would go on to be recontextualised in metaphorical language about the body and 'spiritual' behaviour enabling their ongoing survival in Christianity.

We can do a great deal with things such as this – different, chaotic and contradictory gender perceptions of Jesus and the upheaval of households in Galilee, as well as shifting attitudes towards women and the readjustment and ignoring of these traditions in the development of Christianity through elite women might be one example. The development of Christology is another. But hopefully we can at least acknowledge the idea about how historical chaos generates different emphases and can recontextualise early traditions for their reuse or abandonment in ways removed from their past.

5. Concluding Remarks: Back to the Future

An extreme example of making unexpected connections across time would be those opening quotations from Badiou and Žižek about Jesus plus Paul equals Marx plus Lenin. From what has been discussed so far there are in fact hints that this anachronistic formula has something to it. After all, the earliest Jesus tradition *does* seem to point to a better world and Paul *does* come along controversially reinterpreting the Master's message while carrying out the hard work and establishing the communities. And now the remarkable use of Paul among thinkers such as Badiou and Žižek has Paul doing just this and more: Paul is a thinker pushing for a radical universality in implicit or explicit opposition to Rome and its empire. This reading has obvious affinities with the recent trend that reads Paul as an explicitly or implicitly, or even indifferent, anti-imperial figure in more conventional New Testament studies.

And yet did not Jesus' ideas, Paul's letters and Christian theology become Empire? The radical transformation of the past, the shaking off of particular identities, the idea of neither Jew nor Greek, male nor female, slave nor free *in Christ* (Gal. 3.28) meant that everyone could now be placed under the umbrella of a Christian Empire. Rome effectively developed, rightly or wrongly, these ideas and Christianity became central to a theocracy. This is not simply an abstract reading of Christianity, as if the misguided and power hungry somehow hijacked the 'original' meaning, as the implication of the seemingly benign Gal. 3.28 would already suggest. On the contrary, as studies of the presentation of Jesus in Mark and Revelation in particular have shown, critiques of imperial power in earliest Christian texts were done through absorbing and mimicking the language and structures of power.[59] We likewise see this in our 'Lenin' figure, Paul. It is more than likely that Paul looks forward to some kind of theocracy. In the famous passage from Phil. 2:6-11 we learn that the lowly crucified one will be exalted above all names 'so that at the name of Jesus every knee should bend, in heaven and on earth and under the earth and every tongue should confess that Jesus Christ is Lord' (Phil. 2:10-11). And what is also significant about this is that New Testament scholars, including historical Jesus scholars, can accept Paul's rhetoric and, if anything, intensify it. For example, N.T. Wright, one of the most vocal proponents of the view that Jesus was declared in contrast

---

[59] T.B. Liew, 'Tyranny, Power and Might: Colonial Mimicry in Mark's Gospel', *JSNT* 73, 1999, pp. 7-31; T.B. Liew, *Politics of Parousia: Reading Mark Inter(con)textually* (Leiden: Brill, 1999); S.D. Moore, *Empire and Apocalypse: Postcolonialism and the New Testament* (Sheffield: Sheffield Phoenix Press, 2006)

to Caesar by Paul and the early Christians (though his rhetoric seems to be softening), may see the proclamation of resurrection as a 'politically revolutionary doctrine'.[60] However, even when discussing anti-imperialist rhetoric he likewise discusses (and presumably endorses) imperialist language as a replacement: 'his people are now a "colony of heaven",' claimed Wright, 'an advance guard of the project to bring the whole world under the sovereign and saving rule of Israel's God'.[61]

So where does this leave us? The Gospel tradition has both reactionary and revolutionary tendencies, which co-exist right from the beginning. It has material that is largely alien to contemporary political thinking, irrespective of whether people continue to make the Gospels palatable. That, I think, is an honest reading of the Gospel tradition and reconstructions of the Gospel tradition. However, does it make it redundant? No. The Gospel tradition may or may not be 'applicable' in its entirety but understanding it partly as the 'sigh of the oppressed creature' does give us insight into the ways human beings negotiate historical change. The Otherness of religious belief, whether we like it or not, whether ancient or modern, must be taken seriously if we want to understand the structure of power and social injustice – and to find ways of challenging them both without resorting to the age-old tendency of replacing one system of dominance with another.

[60] N.T. Wright, *The Resurrection of the Son of God* (London: SPCK, 2003), p. 816.
[61] Wright *Resurrection*, pp. 568-69.

Questions and Discussion Starters

1. "Borg's mystical, Buddhist-esque Jesus effectively ends up looking internally, the ultimate capitalist subject". Do you agree with Crossley's implicit argument that many contemporary constructions of Jesus more honestly reflect the neo liberalism of some theologians? How does this sit alongside the Jesus we encounter in the gospels?

2. Can the distinction between a very Jewish Jesus and a Jesus who transcends his Jewish identity be sustained?

3. If the Jesus story and religions in general are used in part to describe and analyse social, economic and political change, what for you are the main lessons to be drawn from an honest portrayal of Jesus? Is he the true radical and what might this mean?

Being Honest in the Church?

Revd Canon Professor Martyn Percy

What does it mean to be honest to the church today? The church in every age has faced fundamental challenges. Many would cite the challenge of secularisation or consumerism in our time as one of the tougher trials the church has had to negotiate. I am not so sure, however. But I do think there are two distinct challenges facing the church today.

The first of these is simple: distraction. It is easy to get deflected from the main purpose of the church through divisive debates. And no one can seriously imagine that the public mission of the church has been helped by recent debates on sexuality and gender. But perhaps, paradoxically, constant talk of mission and growth is also a distraction. No one denies the urgency of mission, and also for the church to address issues of numerical growth.

But the church does not exist to grow. It exists to glorify God and follow Jesus Christ. After which it may grow; or it may not. But it is imperative that faithfulness is always put before any search for success. Indeed, for the vast majority of the population of England, church-talk of mission and numbers tends to drive away far more people than it ever draws near.

Evelyn Underhill, writing to Archbishop Lang on the eve of the 1930 Lambeth Conference of the Anglican Communion, reminded him that the world was not especially hungry for what the church was immediately preoccupied with. Underhill put it sharply in her letter: 'may it please your Grace...I desire to humbly suggest that the interesting thing about religion is God; and the people are hungry for God'.

So what is the second biggest or most fundamental problem facing the church? In Daniel Hardy and David Ford's seminal book *Jubilate: Theology in Praise* (1984), the authors ask precisely this question. You can imagine the question cropping up at a clergy training gathering. Groups of clergy huddled together in groups would hardly pause: the problems nominated could be almost anything: sexuality, gender, the lack of authority or clarity, and so forth. Take your pick. The discussion could rumble on for days.

But Hardy and Ford say that the biggest problem facing the church, is 'coping with the overwhelming abundance of God...' The idea that we are struggling to cope with God's overwhelming abundance might come as a surprise, and possibly a shock. This is just what Hardy and Ford wish to confront us with. For at the heart of the gospel is a God who can give more than we can ask or desire, who gives without counting the cost. A God who gives in almost immeasurable portions: the nets burst; the cup runs over; he comes that we should have life, and life abundant; manna falls; springs rise; deserts bloom.

That said, and when it comes to having vision for shaping the church in the twenty-first century, there is often lively debate on what 'models' of secular organisation might be followed. The church often supposes that by discerning the kinds of secular leadership that seem to work, and identifying which organisations have been apparently successful, the church might benefit in turn.

But just suppose the church is more like an institution, and less like an organisation. Understanding the difference is arguably vital for leadership and management. Organisations are bodies that are free to adapt their identity and focus in order to survive and flourish. Nokia, for example, is a Finnish company that makes and markets mobile phones. But it began its life in the nineteenth century trading in rubber wellington-boots and tractor tyres were amongst its first products. In terms of identity, Nokia is what the theorist Philip Selznick (1919-2010) would identify as an organisation. Nokia exists to succeed and make money. Mobile phones are a means to that end, as rubber was earlier. Nokia are free to change their focus any time so long as that turns a profit and pleases the shareholders.

Institutions, in contrast, have different purposes. They are there to propagate their values from one generation to the next. Crucially, observes Selznick, good institutions should do this independently of the popularity of those values. The church is clearly more like an institution than an organisation. It embodies the life of Jesus in times of penury and persecution, as well as in revival. What it cannot do is to try and change its focus. It risks losing its identity if it does.

Most dioceses now live in the hinterland between organisational and institutional identity. Snappy strap-lines, logos and branding all suggest an appreciable attempt at creating a sharper distinctiveness. 'Growing upwards, inwards, outwards...' for example, may well provide a focus for cohesion and energising. So might 'Committed to Growth' or 'Going for Growth' – two contrasting mottos for different dioceses in the Church of England at present. 'Transform' is the most commonly used word in the thirty or so Church of England dioceses that have strap-lines. The words 'Jesus' and 'Love' do not appear in any strap-line.

Strap-lines are very much the tools of marketing for organizations. They belong to the same genre as 'Coke adds life' or Vodafone's 'power to you'. The strap-lines exist to engender publicity and popularity. (My personal favourite is, however: 'the Church of England: Serving the Nation with a Slight Air of Superiority Since 597')

Some welcome the relatively rapid adoption of new managerial and growth-related thinking in the church. Some do not. Indeed, the range of opinions indicates that the church may still be rather unsure of its moorings here. Are the vogue-ish organisational theories currently shaping the church a season in the desert, a stopover in Babylon, or the proverbial sojourn in the Promised Land? As with most divisive issues in Anglicanism, there are at least three campfires of opinion. We know we are in transit – the church always is. But we are unsure as to whether the next gate is for a departure or an arrival.

So, rebranding and re-launching is fine for organisations seeking to maintain a customer base and grow new markets. But in contrast, this can be rather unsettling for institutions, often cultivating initiative-weariness. Furthermore, in constantly trying to remind the public of their identity and purpose, institutions can risk looking a little desperate, undermining rather than instilling confidence.

Organisations not only look outwards in their restless search for success. They also look inwards, scrutinising for efficiency and productivity. Management comes to the fore here; but it is usually the servant of growth. Typically, the character of managerialism is absorbed with strategies, reviews and the adoption of SMART(er) criteria (i.e., reviewing performance in relation to goals that are specific, measurable, attainable, relevant and time bound – with the addition of evaluation and re-evaluation in recent literature). The church, like education and healthcare, has begun to adopt some of this thinking. Yet none of this resolves the ambiguous nature of ministry: describing it, defining it and then trying to assess its impact remains a tricky conundrum. Apparent success cannot be confused with faithfulness. Clear aims, objectives and outcomes, no matter how appealing, are not to be confused with wisdom.

Robert Towler and Anthony Coxon, in *The Fate of the Anglican Clergy: A Sociological Study* (Routledge, 1979) understood something of the ambiguity of the ministerial role for modern clergy. Their articulation of the issues of identity and function remain relevant. They describe ministry not as work, a profession, or as labour – but as an 'occupation'. It is a rather quaint word, granted. But an 'occupation' is something that consumes time, energy and lives, but is not paid or recognised as 'work' in the way that the secular world understands the term.

This, they argued, made ministry increasingly uncommon – a sphere of activity where remuneration is no longer linked to the value of the endeavour – either for practitioners or for the public at large. They likened ministers to poets, artists or philanthropists. It was hard to say, in other words, how time was spent, to what end, and whether the efforts were 'measurable' or 'valuable'. Much like ministry, really. It is more difficult to understand its value in today's world, even though public and representative functions remain highly visible, symbolic and appreciated (e.g., funerals, weddings, etc.).

To be sure, better organisation is important for mission and ministry. But perhaps more could be said for the concept of 'occupation' in relation to ministry, rather than it being 'work'. Clergy and lay leaders are to be occupied with God. And then to be pre-occupied with the people and places that are given into our care. To dwell amongst, care for and love people and places – as Christ himself occupied the world.

Leadership, it is often said, is doing the right thing; and management is about doing things right. The church needs both, of course. But it is perhaps not unfair to say that the church of the post-war years has moved from being over-led and under-managed to being over-managed and under-led. Kenneth Thompson addresses this in his (catchily-titled!) *Bureaucracy and Church Reform: The Organizational Response of the Church of England to Social Change – 1880-1965* (OUP, 1970). His core thesis was that our post-war internal organisational reforms have been driven by two major external forces.

The first, affecting the church in the late nineteenth and early twentieth centuries, was the differentiation of institutions as they became more specialized in their functions. The church, for example, ceased to run adoption services in the way that it once did – or hospitals, universities and colleges, for that matter.

The second to affect the church was an increased emphasis on rationality, accountability and productivity – such that we are increasingly pre-occupied with immediate, empirical and pragmatic ends. In other words, we try to justify our value through measuring success, and then driving that success by the criteria we chose to measure it by.

But what is often neglected by focusing on the measurable are more nebulous and extensive forms of engagement in public ministry. Prophetic engagement with issues of justice and peace, for example, may suffer: this can be time-consuming, and may not yield any immediate 'measurable results'. Pastoral work too, is hard to quantify and measure. In all of this, the organisational-managerial star tends to rise, whilst that of the institutional-leadership wanes.

There are some ironies here. Bureaucracies and ideologies that support the legitimization of the organisational-managerial quickly sprout into being. This means 'institutions' shift to becoming smaller, rationalised 'organisations'. The movement from the leadership of institutions to management of organisations follows, even though the rhetoric of 'leadership' continues. Indeed, 'leadership-speak' often becomes more prevalent at this point. There have been more books on church leadership published in the last fifty years than in the whole of Christian history. There are more books on leadership in the English language than all books available in Portuguese!

The heart of the matter is this. By treating the church as an organisation, we may not be turning the church into a more efficient, productive body. Rather, we may be slowly encumbering our clergy, lay leaders and churches with layers of administration and managerial processes, built around the quantification of expectations, and their eventual concretization. Put sharply, one's value to the organisation increasingly lies in being able to demonstrate *measurable* growth.

Yet for most ministers, this only tends to produce slowly rising levels of anxiety and disenchantment. Ironically, this causes the church to search for even stronger forms of management, together with rationalizing and efficiencies that will deliver a reinvigorated popularity and measurable growth. However, we may be running serious risks in constantly talking up the prospects for growth, whilst on the ground the situation is one of escalating complex patterns of churchgoing, coupled to increasingly stretched resources, fewer stipendiary ministers, and ever-greater pressures on clergy and churches.

To be clear, I believe that our churches need managing, growing and re-organising more than ever. The Church is clearly a broad, deep, dense institution that needs *some* organisation. But it is not a flagging organisation in search of a new, more appealing identity.

Yet for us as a church today, the presenting problem appears to be declining numbers in our congregations. Ergo, an urgent emphasis on numerical church growth must be the answer. Right, surely? But wrong, actually. The first priority of the church is to follow Jesus Christ. This may be a costly calling, involving denial, depletion and death. Following Jesus may not lead us to any numerical growth. The first priority of the church is to love the Lord with all our heart, mind, soul and strength, and our neighbours as ourselves [Lk. 10: 25]. There is no greater commandment. So the numerical growth of the church cannot be a greater priority than the foundational mandate set before us by Jesus.

It was Karl Barth who observed, more than fifty years ago, that the true growth of the church is not to be thought of in mainly extensive terms, but rather those that are intensive. He argued that the vertical (or intensive) growth of the church – in both height and depth in relation to God – does not necessarily lead to any extensive numerical growth. He added that 'we cannot, therefore, strive for vertical renewal merely to produce a wider audience'. Barth concluded that if the Church and its mission were used only as a means of extensive growth, the inner life of the church loses its meaning and power: 'the church can be fulfilled only for its own sake, and then – unplanned and unarranged – it will bear its own fruits'. [*Church Dogmatics*, 1958]

That would seem to settle the matter. Moreover, many parish clergy, and those working in all kinds of sector ministries, already know this to be true. The church does not exist to grow exponentially. Mission is deeper than that. The church exists to be the body of Christ. The pastoral theologian Eugene Petersen once commented that the one thing he has learned in mission and ministry is how complex measurable growth can be. Here, Petersen draws on the theologian, essayist, poet and farmer, Wendell Berry. Petersen says that under Berry's tutelage he has learnt that 'parish work is every bit as physical as farm work: it is about *these* people, at *this* time under *these* conditions' (see *Under the Unpredictable Plant*, 1992).

The pastoral turn towards an agrarian motif is arresting. Jesus told a number of parables about growth, and they are all striking for their simplicity and surprise, especially the allegory of the sower [Mt. 13: 3-9, etc]. This parable probably should be the template for all Diocesan Mission Action Plans. For what Jesus is saying to the church is this: have regard to your neighbour's context and conditions.

So, you might work in a parish with the richest soil, where every seed planted springs to life. The seasons are kind; the vegetation lush; the harvest plentiful. But some places are stony ground; and faithful mission and ministry in that field might be picking out the rocks for several decades. Others labour under conditions where the seeds are often destroyed before they can ever germinate. Or perhaps the weather is extreme in other places, and here we may find that although initial growth is quick, it seldom ever lasts.

The question the parable throws back to the church is this: what kind of growth can you expect from the ground and conditions you work with? And this is where our current unilateral emphasis on numerical church growth can be so demoralising and disabling. Is it really the case that every leader of numerical church growth is a more spiritually faithful and technically gifted pastor than their less successful neighbour? The parable says 'no' to this. It implies that some churches labour in harsh conditions; some fairer. So be wise to the different contexts in which our individual and collective ministries take place.

I mention this for one very obvious reason. If we continue to place the heterodoxy of numerical growth at the heart of the church, we risk eroding our character, and our morale. Some will argue, no doubt, that if you aim at nothing, you'll hit it every time. Better to have a target and a plan than to just keep plodding on. Maybe. But the Charge of the Light Brigade (1854) had vision, courage, objectives, and some strategy; these were not in short supply. But the rest, as they say, is history. So the key to understanding numerical church growth might be to engage in some deeper and more discerning readings of our contexts – the very soil we seek to nourish and bless, so the seeds can flourish. This will usually be more a complex piece of work than simply announcing another new vision or plan for mission. The pun is intended here: there is work to be done on the ground.

It is hard to imagine a Michael Ramsey, William Temple or Edward King – or for that matter, a John Robinson or David Jenkins – receiving preferment in the current climate. If all leaders must now make obeisance before the altar of numerical church growth, we will erode our character and muffle our mission. The veneration of growth squeezes out the space for broader gifts in leadership that can nourish the church and engage the world.

It is a question of balance. No one can or should say that an emphasis on numerical church growth is wrong. It isn't. The issue is one of proportion. There are no bad foods, only bad diets. And the continued over-emphasis of numerical growth skews the weight and measure in the body of our leadership.

This is a more subtle disproportion than it might at first appear. It was said of the late Cardinal Basil Hume that 'he had the gift of being able to talk to the English about God without making them wish they were somewhere else'. The value of this gift should not be underestimated.

And for our national mission, this is precisely why we need a leadership that incorporates space for the holy and devout; the gentle pastor; the poet and the prophet; the teacher and theologian; and possibly a radical or two for good measure. The church may not always draw near to such leaders. But the nation often does – especially those who don't usually go to church. So for the sake of our national mission, we may want to intentionally develop a broader range of leaders than the very singular objective of numerical church growth will currently allow for.

So to conclude, let us return to numbers. Some of the most recent figures for numerical church growth in the Church of England offer up some surprising anomalies. In the *2010/11 Church Statistics*, many dioceses that had well developed mission strategies showed continuing numerical decline. Only a few did not.

But perhaps the greatest surprise was to discover one diocese that had enjoyed significant numerical growth – a whopping 17 percent in average weekly and usual Sunday attendance. Ironically, this was led by a bishop who had seemingly little in the way of experience in mission and ministry. Like Basil Hume, the bishop had not been a parish priest, and could not tick any of the boxes that indicated he had led any congregation to numerical growth.

The diocese was Canterbury. And the bishop was someone who also had the gift of being able to talk to the English about God. Having the knack of imaginative, reflective and refractive God-talk does indeed intrigue people, who might not otherwise pay any attention to the rumour of God.

So by welcoming some teachers, poets and prophets amongst our leadership, and who point us imaginatively and compellingly to Christ, we might yet discover an even richer, more effective purpose in our mission. And in so doing, also find some other routes to numerical growth along the way.

So to emphasize, there are two simple points being made here. First, let's have less talk about numbers and mission. In talking up the possibilities for numbers, the church is sounding increasingly disingenuous, and almost dishonest. Second, let's have more talk about God – good, honest theology and spirituality.

It's not difficult. As every leader of any political party knows, once you start talking about the need to increase membership, it decreases. But when you start talking about ideas and the fundamental things that matter, people join. Dare one say it? We, as a church, sound like we are out of ideas. And our leaders mostly sound like managers trying to fix the numbers.

This is potentially quite serious for our national mission. As Professor Linda Woodhead's research has recently shown, the vast majority of the population remain well disposed to the Church of England. What puts them off, however, is too much talk from inside the church of money, management and numerical growth. The church – in continuing to stress these concerns – may imagine it is being proactive. But these foci represent reactive responses to wider cultural concerns, which can occlude the deeper character of the church. Correspondingly, it is rare to see an advertisement at the back of a church newspaper seeking a Vicar who will lead a church into deeper theological learning, or open up the riches of contemplative prayer to the wider parish. Our absorption with management and growth dominates our selection processes – from top to bottom.

All of this could be leading us into dangerous forms of cognitive dissonance; the discomfort experienced when we try and hold, simultaneously, two or more conflicting beliefs or values. For example, a sample diocese might set a target of numerically growing their congregations by ten percent over five years. But if the economy is in a downturn, giving in parishes will be hit. Diocesan budgets are often trimmed at this point, and clergy posts frozen. Can you believe in a growing diocese if it is, in fact, in recession? Not easily. Either the facts have to change, or the mindset does.

We may be running serious risks in constantly talking up the prospects for growth, whilst on the ground the situation is one of escalating complex patterns of churchgoing and institutional affiliation, coupled to increasingly stretched resources, fewer stipendiary ministers, and ever-greater pressures on clergy and churches. Measuring quantity as an indicator of quality, and success as a gauge of faithfulness, carries challenges and risks. If our numbers point to decline, but the rallying-cry is still 'Grow!', morale will eventually suffer. As will trust in the realism and vision of the leadership. We may need some deeper discernment here, and some sharper critical-reflection.

We also need to do some work on the maths. In the secular world, one plus one equals two. But counting and adding whole numbers in the church is fuzzy logic. Is the newly baptised infant 'one unit' in terms of believers? Does the person who comes every week, but has more doubt than faith count as 'one' or a 'half'? Is the regular, but not frequent churchgoer 'one' – or less? Is the person who comes to everything in church, but has a heart of stone, count as one? Or less? We know that God counts generously. The poor, the lame, the sick, the sinners...all seem to be promised a whole, complete seat at God's table in his kingdom, feasting with him.

That's why Jesus was seldom interested in *quantity*; the Kingdom is about small numbers and rich *quality*. Numbers mean so little in true mission. Yet we live in a culture that is obsessed by measuring things numerically, and judging success from this. Fortunately, God is loving and wise enough to tell us lots of counter-cultural stories about numbers: going after one, and leaving ninety-nine, for example. Or dwelling on a single sparrow.

God's maths is different from ours. And God does not easily concur with our cultural obsessions with "growth-equals-success". To be sure, we need leaders who can ride the cultural waves of our time. But we also need other leaders who can *read* the tides, and the deeper cultural currents of our age. Our recent emphasis on numerical church growth – borne largely from fear, not faith – has led us to the unbalanced ascendancy of mission-minded middle managers in our church.

Fifty years on, I wonder what John Robinson would make of the Church of England today, and of Christianity in contemporary culture? I think he'd be surprised by some things. That secularisation, as a thesis, and as reality, is all but dead. That despite serious levels of decline in our national churchgoing, public interest in religion remains strong; and widespread innate spiritual inklings are still very prevalent in society. He'd be concerned about the collapse of theological breadth, depth, competence and confidence in our bishops, and its knock-on effect for broad public theology: church leaders today largely talk to the faithful, with few exceptions. Of the few who do try and offer public God-talk, the results are mixed: courage and confidence is not always matched with wisdom, alas.

So to conclude, let me plant a seed. Let's have less talk about mission and growth; and much more talk about God. Yes, let's talk about God. Then, and only then, might the church actually begin to grow and flourish as a truly public entity – a body receptive to the world it is here for. In short, let us be honest about the church today – to God, and for the world.

Questions and Discussion Starters

1. In your experience does 'the church' function as an institution or as an organisation? Does 'success' matter and how would you define a successful church?

2. What should be the work of church leaders, both ordained and lay?

3. Percy says that the first priority of the church is to follow Christ. What does this mean in its outworkings?

4. If the church is to talk less about numbers and more about God, where might it start?

Being Honest about ourselves

Simon Barrow

What is involved in being honest about ourselves as human beings? What does it mean for responding to the ethical challenges posed by the world we inhabit, shape and rely upon? If honesty is the best policy, what strategies of implementation are needed?

Since 'we' (whoever the 'we' is) are contingent, historical, inculturated and reflexive creatures – what Alasdair MacIntyre refers to in his fine book as *Rational Dependent Animals*,[i] any attempt to address such questions is bound to involve wrestling with the notion of honesty in particular located ways, acknowledging the disabilities and vulnerabilities that make us reliant upon, and interdependent with, others.

The sometimes painful attempt at such reflection in John Robinson's *Honest to God* offers, fifty years on, some helpful, if fitful, resources for doing this. But before I explore some of the themes Robinson raises, and a few he does not, I would like to start at what many take to be the beginning, but which is in fact always a flowing middle.

In the old days we used to call that place 'the dictionary'. For many now it is called Googling. One of the results you get when you put "define: honesty" into the world's largest online search engine is for a company which claims to be "a trusted source for stylish, eco-friendly baby diapers, wipes, bath and body care products." Yes, these days honesty is yet another commoditized product to be bought and sold!

This is clearly not the kind of honesty John Robinson had in mind. His book, whatever you think of it, was the result not merely of a successful marketing strategy in *The Observer* and the *Daily Mirror* (though that went well to an extent which a modern theological author could only dream of), but of struggling with his own shadows, with both the trivialities and agonising features of daily life in donnish Cambridge and inner city south-east London, with the responsibilities of being a bishop for a tribe that is supposed to be non-tribal,[ii] with the vocation of following a Jesus all-too-often imprisoned by the church, and with the joys and disappointments brought on by the desire truthfully to reflect 'transcendence in the midst' for those (himself included) caught up in the sheer jumble of life.

It is surely significant that John Robinson first conceived *Honest to God* during a period of enforced inactivity through a back problem that meant hospitalization and convalescence. Honesty requires patience, patience takes time, and time has also increasingly been reduced to another fiercely fought-over commodity over the past five decades. Robinson worked through several versions of the manuscript before it was finished in 1962 and published by SCM Press in 1963. Twenty years later, the final collection of articles that bear his name, *Where Three Ways Meet*,[iii] includes a series of (for me) almost unbearably moving sermons where he locates his own dying from cancer within the unfolding love of the God in whom he found himself living, moving and having his being – that Johannine 'eternal life in the present' which surely stands at the core of *Honest to God*'s probings (even if many interpreters and critics have not recognized this), and which must therefore be a key part of any attempt to be Honest to Robinson.

Professor Elaine Graham is right to suggest that his book was, to a significant extent, about recovering the essentials of Christian belief in a different mode or register, not ditching them.[iv] The same, I think, goes for Christology, spirituality and morality. The author of *Honest to God* was a conservative radical, not an all-out revolutionary. He was not a prophet of reductionist naturalism, or of the submersion of theological categories into a purely immanentist anthropology, or of a linguistically free-floating religious expressivism (to name just three allegedly 'progressive' or 'radical' directions into which this book has been pressed, by proponents and opponents alike).[v] That he has often been so pressed obviously tells us something about subjectivity in interpretation. It may also point to the cloudiness of thought that can sometimes fall on the most precise mind when it is honestly pushing the boundaries of the sayable (which will always be the case with God). But if that is a fault – and over the years many reviewers have not spared their scorn for the unevenness of *Honest to God* – it is surely more forgivable than a too-ready projection of our own wishes onto others. Which brings me to my first main point:

1. Honesty about ourselves requires us to acknowledge the limits of our experience as well as our understanding.

It is dangerous to try to speak too much for others or to put words in their mouths. We have to learn to speak for ourselves, afresh. This is what John Robinson sought to do. It is much less straightforward than it sounds. To do so we have, for example, to make serious efforts to discern, learn and migrate with the languages of others (in a way that, for example, recent debates sparked by the so-called New Atheism almost never do, on any side). We have to see something of the relation between our context(s) and quite different ones. (In an important sense, both the strengths and weaknesses of *Honest to God* are the result of John Robinson 'crossing worlds' in intellectual, pastoral and sociological terms – though that may not be immediately obvious from the style in which it is written). We have to factor into our talking and thinking the impact of the non-appearance of the people who could be in the conversation, but who are not (something an able-bodied, middle aged, middle class, educated, relatively un-impoverished, white, heterosexual Christian male such as myself should not be allowed to forget).

We also have to learn to say what we mean as well as mean what we say, and to acknowledge the difficulty of that. (When someone tells us that we should just "be ourselves" this is, in my experience, not at all simple. It is much easier to pretend to be someone or something else than to admit that we frequently struggle to know ourselves, let alone others). For example, I am still tempted to enter into endless qualifications within what I say and write, but I have come to recognize that, apart from making life difficult for other people, this is mainly an exercise in trying to defend myself and my opinions from anticipated attacks. In the long run, however, it is surely more fruitful (if also more risky) to try to make awkward friends with 'the other' *qua* other (in myself, too), rather than to ward him, her or it off.

2. Honesty about ourselves requires a renewed sensitivity towards the impact of language on who we are and how we think.

Since we are language-borne and language-bound creatures, the world is always conveyed as we tell it, and learning to make better representations of what we encounter and are encountered by is crucial to avoiding the deceits (including the self-deceit) that imperils honesty and much else beside.

In this context, John Robinson's rejection of the distant, imperial, *deus ex machina* God is morally as well as metaphysically and theologically significant. "Death is turned into life, not by a power that overpowers things (like the god of omnipotence-theology), but by the kingdom of 'weak forces' (like the God of Jesus and the *via crucis*)," declares John D Caputo.[vi] However, while *Honest to*

God clearly recognised the difficulty with popular rhetoric about God, its major reparative strategy – opting for an inward metaphor drawn from depth psychology at the expense of a spatial one drawn from mythological cosmology, and assuming that the former to be more 'credible' to the 'modern mind' than the latter – was less successful. Among other things, it failed to recognise the inescapability of metaphoric language for God.

Here there is a practical, ethical issue bound up in the theological one which requires a short historical *discursus*.[vii] The exponential advance of instrumental reason since the 17th century led to the world being seen in terms of objects ('things'), components, functions and causes. This produced fine technology but also impoverished philosophy. Human beings came, for a while, to be seen as sophisticated, manipulable machines. Armed with this view the first two industrial revolutions produced progress, but also dehumanisation. At the same time, there was a corresponding shift in the meaning of God. Explains Nicholas Lash, in his remarkable book *Holiness, Speech and Silence: Reflections on the Question of God* (which I would see as the worthiest response to John Robinson's theological probings): "The word 'god' once worked rather like the word 'treasure' still does. A treasure is what someone... highly values. And I can only find out what you value by asking you and by observing your behaviour... There is no class of object known as 'treasures'... valuing is a relationship."[viii]

However, with the dominance of instrumental reason, 'gods' became, correspondingly, 'things' of a certain kind, a 'divine' one. Analogously, the 'home territory' of God-understanding shifted from worship (the assignment of value) to description (the assignment of properties). It became a metaphysical enterprise rather than a matter of appropriate relationship.

This shift of meaning and affection fundamentally corrupted and disabled the modern comprehension of 'God' – because God is, logically and necessarily, beyond definition (delimiting) and categorisation. God is most definitely not a 'thing' belonging to a class of things called 'gods'. "Christians, Jews, Muslims and atheists all have this, at least, in common: that none of them believe in gods", says Lash. Therefore religions are best considered 'schools' in which people learn properly to relate to God appropriately precisely by not worshipping any thing – not the world nor any part, person, dream, event or memory in it. [ix]

God is rendered 'unbelievable' for many today because we have forgotten this. Lash again: People "simply take for granted that the word 'god' names a natural kind, a class of entity. There are bananas, traffic lights, human beings, and gods. Or perhaps not: on this account... 'theists' are people who suppose the class of gods to have at least one member... 'atheists' are those who think that, in the real world, the class of 'gods' is, like the class of 'unicorns', empty." This is a basic category mistake with lethal consequences. As Denys Turner says, commenting on Aquinas: "In showing God to 'exist' reason shows that we no longer know what 'exists' means."[x] The point he makes was not discovered by Tillich or Bultmann. In its classical origins it is rather traditional and creatively orthodox.[xi]

Now an overwrought instrumental, objectifying reason (the kind that leads us morally and aesthetically, in Oscar Wilde's famous aphorism, "to know the price of everything and the value of nothing") also readily subjugates us to the notion that technical and abstract language ('ineffability', 'transcendence' and so on) is inherently superior to the concrete anthropomorphic imagery of biblical thought, attributing the latter to the simple-minded. By the time you get to the end of the first paragraph of the first chapter of *Honest to God*, St Luke has been accused of depicting Christ in "the crudest terms" and the Athenians of holding "primitive notions" of the divine through the application of figurative, anthropomorphic speech. Yet as John Robinson reminds us in many of his biblical exegeses, poor reading is not absolved by blaming the author.

For the reality is that *all* language (including analytic and philosophical terminology) is humanly generated. Moreover, everything we say of God, in whatever register, is metaphorically said, and speech or writing that makes us conscious of this – not least entering the other world that is the Bible – is actually less likely to deceive itself, and us, by attempting a 'fix' on 'what God is'. Or, indeed, what we are. When we speak of God we can only refer and invoke, never describe or capture. The epistemic modesty and good faith that this requires may infuriate both Richard Dawkins and a certain kind of Southern Baptist pastor, but it should not disturb those open to the possibility of what Robinson calls "the unconditioned in the conditioned" and the one Rowan Williams speaks of as "the wholly non-competitive other."

When it comes to our engagement with the language of the Bible, of course, the delights and deceits of language are very closely bound together – and the temptations this affords may be an even greater problem for modern Christianity than some of the broader issues about God-talk. This leads into my next major point.

3. Honesty about ourselves requires *metanoia*, conversion, a change of heart – not self-aggrandisement.

Some years ago I was involved with a conference which, if memory serves me correctly, was held here in Swanwick. It was entitled *Christian adult educators: Prophets or Pharisees?* Our keynote speaker did not make himself instantly popular with all the participants by having the honesty to question the set-up proposed by the title. "I suspect," he said (and I am purely paraphrasing here), "that in choosing the alternative roles of prophet or Pharisee, we adult educators have already decided, first, that this is a matter of 'good guys' versus 'bad guys', and second that we are the 'good guys'. The 'good guys', of course, are the prophets. They are radicals, they speak truth to power. The 'bad guys' are the Pharisees. They tie up people in religious red tape."

But this way of putting things might be deeply self-serving. For a start, are we really prophets? Being a prophet isn't a job description that we make up. It's a calling. And the real four-star biblical prophets don't sit around congratulating themselves after preaching a bit of a daring sermon, they ended up in jail or on the end of a gibbet for challenging the false religious-political system – the kind of enterprise that got Jesus killed. Equally, the Pharisees, though they get a bad press in the Gospels, were not necessarily the religious thought-police they sometimes get presented as, it has been suggested. Indeed there is a decent argument to be made that Jesus was making arguments within rather than simply against Pharisaism. In essence those identified with this group were trying to make the Law accessible to ordinary people and so enable them to be included rather than excluded. The manipulative operators are the ones we hear about, but lazily dismissing a whole group of people because of the behaviour of a few, and elevating ourselves on the back of them, is the kind of thing the *Daily Mail* and the *Daily Express* do. It is hardly something Christian educators should be commending or practising.

Perhaps this little example of radical Christian hubris reflects a common tendency within human life to see the problem as other people and the solution as ourselves. The Gospel reminds us that other people starts with us, and that at some level we all need rescuing from ourselves such that we can be restored in relationship – to paraphrase Bishop Peter Selby, a former president of what is now Modern Church.[xii] What might that look like and mean?

Back in 1984, I spent time visiting basic Christian communities in Italy; dissidents from the Vatican working out their faith in council blocks, high streets and factories. I vividly remember a Bible study in a block of flats in Turin. It was on John chapter 3, and Jesus' words to Nicodemus about the need to be born again – a classic evangelical text. A young woman who had just joined the group, which routinely ended with a eucharist by making the remaining elements part of a feast to which all in the block were invited, suggested her own reading. "I am a midwife," she said. "This talk of a second birth is puzzling to me. But I wonder if what Jesus is getting at is that when we are first born into this world, everything has to be done for us and the world revolves around us. To be re-born, then, is to be born away from ourselves and towards others, to be opened up to the world and to God instead of being self-centred."[xiii]

I still think that is one of the best interpretations I have heard, and a clear challenge to us. This woman did not think of herself as 'religious' (as tied to what we now call 'organised religion') but she described herself as "becoming a Christian" in learning how her life and those of others could be turned around by taking up the invitation to join with them in developing practices of welcome, generosity, forgiveness and sharing. It was on this path, sustained by liturgy, that Christ and God started to become meaningful for her. She had been encountered by the one Robinson, following Bonhoeffer, called the Man for Others, and in her own words had begun to discover "what it is to be full of life". Again, not a new insight or experience. As Saint Irenaeus is supposed to have put it: "The glory of God is a living human being; and to be alive consists in beholding God." Not as object, but as transformative relationship. It is in acknowledging our fracturedness and seeking wholeness that we begin to regain the capacity to be honest about others, the world and ourselves.

4. Honesty about ourselves requires us to confront 'institutional truth'.

'Institutional truth' is a term first used by the American political economist John Kenneth Galbraith to describe the self-deceptions of the powerful masquerading as honest assessment.[xiv] It is the truth, the facts of the situation, as rendered palatable and usable by Wall Street, Goldman Sachs, the military-industrial complex – and, latterly, the apostles of neoliberal austerity economics who tell us that the debt system that has enriched a few and impoverished many can only be healed by continuing to make the poor pay while we bail out the rich; that there is money for warfare, but not for welfare. Of course, tackling these issues is complex and multilayered. But recognizing the deceptions that disguise themselves as revelation is a critical first step to addressing the real problems. [xv]

According to Jesus, "the truth will set you free". But what if the reality which the truth points us to is too much for human beings to bear (T. S Eliot)? What if there is good money to be made out of imprisonment? Against a harsh backdrop such as this, John Robinson's chapter on 'the new morality' at the end of *Honest to God*, or his book *Christian Freedom in a Permissive Society* (SCM Press, 1970) might look well-meaning but a little thin fifty years on – and far too obsessed with sex. Figuring out what the most loving thing is for different people in a specific situation may not get you very far at all in the face of wider, institutional intractability.

What happens when lies have become enshrined as truth? What then for Fletcher's situational ethic? How, for example, could we use it to confront what Walter Wink calls an endemic "myth of redemptive violence" (the deeply rooted idea that the only way to address violence is with more violence)?[xvi] Is liberalism enough to sustain liberality when the going gets really tough, asks Peter Selby?[xvii] Here John Robinson perhaps missed a different trick from Bonhoeffer, whose fragmentary ethics was formed in that least promising of circumstances: a world full of Nazis.

In that context, Dietrich Bonhoeffer once declared words to the effect that "a truth on the lips of a liar is of far less moral worth than a lie on the lips of a truthful man."[xviii] This was no relativizing ethic, but a reminder that truth (and the honesty that makes it possible) is embodied first in truthful lives – those oriented to defending life as gift, rather than manipulating or discarding it as possession. In the Abwehr (the German military intelligence organization he joined in 1941, and from which he operated as a double agent) functionaries spoke mundane truths every day. But their lives were fully disposed to supporting a Lie. Bonhoeffer and others, by contrast, found themselves needing to tell routine (and sometimes spectacular) untruths in order to subvert the culture of that lie. To hide Jews, for example. Were they being honest or dishonest? Let us not forget that the real truth at stake in a Nazified 'normality' was not words, but life itself.

None of this came easily to the conventional, upright Bonhoeffer. Nor did he try to gloss it with an easy theological rationale. What his observation about people of the truth and people of the lie points to is the claim of an absolute condition of love in a culture that has rendered itself blind to such a claim. To see this as straightforward situationalism is entirely mistaken. At its deepest level it is the opposite of that: a challenge to resist the false integrity of the irresistible will to power. Pitted against such forces, honesty in the routine sense may *not* always be the best policy – though there is, of course, the story told by the Dutch pietist Corrie Ten Boom, who when asked whether there were any Jews in a particular household truthfully said, "they're under the table". Her interrogators reportedly laughed at such a preposterous notion and left. [xix]

5. Honesty about ourselves requires frameworks of mutual accountability and a continual remaking of relationships.

Honesty, the ability to face and bear truthfulness, is not simply something that an autonomous rational subject can dream up and put into action on his or her own. It resides in, and as, a set of virtues that have to be nurtured, developed and extended in community. If the church is to be of any earthly use (which is to say of real heavenly value), the cultivation of alternative ways of living that embody the radical impact of transformative love (*metanoia*, to use the biblical word) has to be at its heart.

Deontological ethics, which Robinson scrutinizes critically, is based on rules. But these only finally work if they are inscribed on the heart, interpreted by love and finally superseded by both, as St Paul reminds us. Consequentialist (particularly utilitarian) ethics supposedly deals in 'what works', but also in calculated winners and losers along with limited, majoritarian notions of happiness. By contrast, a contemporary version of virtue ethics concerns itself with building persons and communities of character, formed to resist the blandishments of a consumerist approach to life, and oriented towards sustaining the kind of habits that make things like peacemaking and restorative justice practical – both on a small scale, and as the basis for rethinking larger interventions and policies. This is something which Ekklesia, the think-tank I help direct, is especially concerned to work on.[xx]

In his chapter on 'Worldly Holiness', John Robinson cites extensively, especially on recasting prayer, from *Only One Way Left*, by George MacLeod, founder of the Iona Community, of which I am honoured to be an associate member.[xxi] This book is based on a memorable series of the Cunningham Lectures delivered in 1954 at New College, Edinburgh, and repeated as the Auburn Lectures in Union Theological Seminary, New York. Disturbed by the church's comparative failure to face up to the crises of the mid-20th century, not least urban poverty and the proliferation of weapons of mass destruction, MacLeod said that the Christianity had become so 'religious' that it had forgotten that God's coming in human form was the locus and shape of its vocation, and that the Christian faith can only be properly comprehended and practised in community. He provocatively claimed: "The great criticism of the Church [in the West] today is that no one wants to persecute it, because there is nothing very much to persecute it about."

His answer was to look at how local church congregations could be reshaped into communities of transformation. The Iona Community today, as a dispersing and gathering international network, based in Scotland, seeks to render this vision by rebuilding common life, working for justice and peace, uniting work and worship and honouring the sacred in (rather than apart from) the secular. For members, it involves the discipline of accounting to one another for the use of money and resources, as well as a commitment to prayer and study. The difficult honesty of the Community's economic discipline is perhaps the clearest and most counter-cultural sign of what mutual accountability and the remaking of relationships means in concrete terms.[xxii] As the wonderfully irascible American theological ethicist Stanley Hauerwas has said: "rightly understood, the church does not have a social ethic, it *is* a social ethic." Or not, as the case may be.

6. Honesty about ourselves requires rooted radicalism to enable us to face the challenge of change.

The last chapter of *Honest to God*, 'Recasting the Mould', begins by noting the demise of Christendom, the era of what we might call 'the Church of Power', and by posing a serious question about the future of 'organised Christianity' *per se*. While Robinson has proved wrong so far about the overall demise of religiosity in the world, he rightly predicted the continual demise of the institutional church. In honestly seeking to face the truth of this situation, he ends up once again returning to the necessity for radicalism – by which he means the nurturing of healthy roots (Latin: *radix*) in such a way that the courage and capacity for deep change becomes possible.[xxiii]

Here being honest about ourselves entails acknowledging what elsewhere Simone Weil describes as "the need for roots". Uprooting everything would abandon a rich inheritance that still nourishes us; mere reform in the face of a changing world would fail to take seriously the need to reshape what we have inherited in a way that does real justice to past, present and future. As the territory shifts, to stand still is not to stay in the same place but to go backwards.

"The true radical," Robinson writes, "is the [one] who continually subjects the Church to the judgement of the Kingdom, to the claims of God ... in the world which the Church exists to serve." Or as he quotes Bonhoeffer asking: "[I]n what way are we the *Ekklesia*, 'those who are called forth', not conceiving of ourselves religiously as specially favoured, but as wholly belonging to the world?"

Much has changed in the past fifty years, but perhaps that is the most radical question of all, because it calls us to immersive action based on the call of the Other in God and neighbour, and a recognition of the need for a major reorientation of the church after Christendom,[xxiv] not simply the reordering of our conceptual frameworks of understanding.

Questions and Discussion Starters

1. How much are we willing to engage deeply with those very different from ourselves in order to understand ourselves more honestly?

2. Does being a 'language born creature' inevitably point to a provisionality of all that we say about ourselves and about God?

3. 'To be reborn...is to be born away from ourselves and towards others'. Do you agree?

4. Do we need a framework of community and mutual accountability in order to be truthful?

i   Alasdair McIntyre, *Dependent Rational Animals: Why Human Beings Need the Virtues* (Duckworth Press, 1999).

ii   On this theme, see the fine little book by Peter Selby, *BeLonging: Challenge to a tribal church* (SPCK, 1991).

iii   John Robison, *Where Three Ways Meet: Last essays and sermons* (SCM Press, 1987). The 'three ways' are theological enquiry, biblical investigation, and engagement with current affairs.

iv   This comment was made in her introductory remarks to the conference at which this paper was delivered.

v   My own theological position is one I would describe as 'subversive orthodoxy'. Unlike many who are labelled liberal or progressive, I believe the formularies and arguments of the Christian tradition and the texts of scripture offer substantial, sound resources for engaging, and being engaged by, the contemporary in an ongoing interpretative dialogue.

vi   A theme developed in the remarkable book by John Caputo, *The weakness of God: A theology of the event* (Indiana University Press, 2006).

vii   The following paragraph is a remarkably inadequate summary of part of an important, extensive, sinewy argument from Michael J. Buckley SJ, *At the origins of modern atheism* (Yale University Press, 1987).

viii   Nicholas Lash, *Holiness, speech and silence: Reflections on the question of God* (Ashgate, 2004), pp.14-15.

ix   Simon Barrow, '*What difference does God make today?*' (Ekklesia, July 2007).

x   See Denys Turner, '*On Denying the Right God: Aquinas on Atheism and Idolatry*', *Modern Theology*, volume 20 number 1 (January 2004).

xi   Unfortunately, the word 'orthodoxy' has come to mean rigidity and dogmatism in modern popular discourse. It is worth reminding ourselves that it actually comes from two Latin words which first and foremost denote a rightful disposition of thankfulness (praise), seeing life as God's gift to be savoured, rather than a possession to be grasped. This helpful, relational understanding is developed well by Rowan Williams at the end of his magisterial *Arius: Heresy and tradition* (Eerdmans, 20012), and by Kenneth Leech in the third chapter of *Subversive Orthodoxy: Traditional faith and radical commitment* (Anglican Book Centre, Canada, 1992).

xii   Peter Selby, *Rescue: Jesus and salvation today* (SPCK, 1995).

xiii   Simon Barrow, '*Rediscovering the church in the mission of the uninvited*' (CMS paper, 1984).

xiv   Doyen economist J. K. Galbraith first used the term publicly in 1991, during a graduation address to students at Smith College, a private liberal arts college for women located in Northampton, Massachusetts, USA.

xv   A good, short economic and philosophical analysis of the deceptive myths that underlie austerity ideology and neoliberalism can be found in Ann Pettifor, *Just Money: How society can break the despotic power of finance* (Prime Economics, 2014).

xvi   Walter Wink, '*Facing the Myth of Redemptive Violence*' (Ekklesia, republished 21 May 20132).

xvii   Liberality is vital in life and in theology, but as Bonhoeffer also knew only too well, despite his wariness of a certain positivism in Barth, when the going gets really tough mere liberalism is not enough. Only the difficult but hopeful realities of incarnation, cross and resurrection will do.

xviii   This sentiment is relayed in the posthumously constructed and edited work *Ethics* (ed. Eberhard Bethge, Macmillan, 1965) as, "It is worse for a liar to tell the truth than for a lover of truth to lie."

[xix] Cornelia ten Boom was a Dutch evangelical Christian who, along with her father and other family members, helped many Jews escape the Nazi Holocaust and was imprisoned for it. See Corrie Ten Boom, *Holocaust Encyclopedia*, United States Holocaust Memorial Museum, Washington, DC – last updated online in November 2013.

[xx] Ekklesia is a Christian political think-tank that works ecumenically, with people of all faiths and none, but is rooted in dissenting and 'peace church' traditions.

[xxi] George F. MacLeod, *Only one way left* (Wild Goose Publications, 2000). First published in 1956.

[xxii] More on the Iona Community: http://iona.org.uk. I am not seeking to idealise this particular experiment in dispersing and gathering Christian community, but it has many lessons to offer. The 'emergent' church movement offers many other examples of consciously discipleship-oriented Christian expressions. See also Stuart Murray, *Church after Christendom* (Paternoster Press, 2005).

[xxiii] John Robinson, *Roots of a Radical* (SCM Press, 1980).

[xxiv] Anabaptist Network, '*Gospel and culture after Christendom*' (http://www.anabaptistnetwork.com/node/609) provides an introduction to some of the major themes and premises of 'Post-Christendom' thinking.

Being Honest about God

Richard Holloway

This is not going to be a lecture. I am not trying to persuade you in or out of anything. I've given that up. I don't stay in any one place myself for very long. So I've no right to fix the place anyone else should establish themselves in. What I want to do is to offer a kind of testimony to where I am and to consider the mysterious business that we think of as religion and the ultimate nature of meaning - if there is any ultimate meaning in the universe. Since I've written my memoir "Leaving Alexandria" I've been going round and round the place and up and down on the earth like Satan because there are book festivals all over the world now. You get a book out and get invited to them. Nearly everywhere I'm asked by one or two members of the audience "Do you still believe in God?" and I sigh and say "It depends upon the god you're talking about". Because one of the things that characterises the story of God is the story of constant revision, abandonment and death and leaving of God, there is a sense in which we've all 'taken leave of God' to quote Don Cupitt, or taken leave of certain gods.

I was priested in the Scottish Church in 1960 and the God of the Scottish Church at that time taught that you got only one shot at marriage because marriage created an indissoluble metaphysical bond and you could only be metaphysically bonded once. So there was no second chance – if you mucked it up or had an affair or the marriage failed, that was it. You were metaphysically welded together in the eyes of God and, when people came to me asking for a second chance, the answer in my church that God had given them was "No!" You had one shot at it and, if you didn't make it, tough. You had to practise celibacy because divorce was institutionalised adultery. I never really believed in that kind of God, but that was the God that I had to officially commit myself to. The God in whom my Church believed in 1960 taught the subordination of women and the impossibility of women receiving the character of ordination. I was brought up as an Anglo-Catholic. Anglo-Catholics believed that in the act of ordination the bishop laid his hands on you and there was mystically inserted into you a substance called the character of ordination. It was a kind of magical ability conferred on you to conjure up in the Eucharist the body and blood of Christ in the bread and wine. And a woman was incapable of receiving that character. There was just no way. If a bishop laid his hands on a woman, it was just a charade. If you ordained a woman you wouldn't be getting the real Jesus when you went to Mass. And it gets worse because, if you had women bishops, you're not getting real priests at all because a woman bishop cannot insert a character of ordination into anyone including a man. So if you start having women bishops you wouldn't ever know whether you're getting the real Jesus around the country. You could go to communion in Blackburn or Brighton and you wouldn't know if the person up there doing the magic had actually got the right to do it. Superstition. But we were taught to believe in the pipeline of grace called the Apostolic Succession. It only came through male hands; it couldn't get through female hands and so forth. There were many examples of that. There was absolutely no way you could debate the possibility that the God of the Scottish Church might approve the possibility for two people of the same sex making physical love to each other. That was not even on the cards.

If we are to be honest about God – which I've been loosely asked to talk about – we have to accept that there is a human history of God - and Karen Armstrong wrote a very fat book outlining God's history. It's a history of constant editing and revising and abandoning. Your church and my church has largely abandoned the God of the 1960's. The only point I'm making at this moment is that the history of God is a history of constant flux and change and abandonment. We need to be honest about that.

Let's go back even further. I was taught, as a young theology student with a bit of a thing about Kierkegaard, that one of the most important lections in the Old Testament was the story of Abraham's almost sacrifice of Isaac. And that this taught a kind of absolute obedience that countermanded any human loyalty. I struggled with that myself as a human being – I would hate to have been the wee boy on the altar with this man, my father, obeying the will of God by sacrificing me. It was a novelist that taught me to see it from Isaac's side. In Jenny Diski's novel, "After These Things", the author sees it from the point of view of the boy being sacrificed in order for the man to demonstrate his absolute obedience to the God he worshipped. What Isaac feels is terror. I suspect that behind that story there is an evolution out of the practice of child sacrifice. When Christian theology uses that story, it has cleansed it, turned it into a kind of metaphor of total obedience, but I suspect it is part of the evolution of this change in the history of God, this moving us away from the understandings into something more human, more adaptable, something we ourselves can more appropriately live with.

Now part of the problem in all of this lies in the secondary aspects of this whole business of theology and God, which is the claim of revelation - those secondary institutions which claim to, as it were, mirror and reflect the meaning and reality of God. Part of the problem is, of course, that the revelatory documents are very old, and that they tend to reflect the values of the time in which the revelation took place. Which is why, in John Hicks' famous typology of realism, critical realism and non-realism, he says there are three attitudes to this. There is an attitude which says there is a real God, a real revelation and we've got to accept and obey it. Critical realists are people who say there was a real God and a real revelation, but we are really screwed up receivers as humans so we cannot claim to have received it accurately and therefore it has to be critically interpreted. So you're in this constant balance between sifting as it were the gold – the real essence of what has been revealed and sifting out the stuff that's adventitious, that's of the time - such as the subordination of women, such as possibly the sacrifice of children.

One of the ways in which we have done this is by increasingly asserting our own moral values against the values that claim to have been revealed, which is why Hicks' third element in his typology is non-realism. This is us, making up our response to the mystery of the universe in which we find ourselves, in which we are set, in which we have been thrown and which obsesses us. Tillich said religion was obsessively asking us the question about the meaning of existence because it doesn't come to us: we didn't come into this world with a manual like a new computer telling us all what it means. We came into this world asking questions about the meaning of our own existence and the meaning of the universe itself. That, passionately addressed, is religion and there's no one way of doing it.

One of the things passionate religionists have done is to challenge passionately the answers they received to the questions they asked about the universe. Diarmaid McCulloch has got a book out – his Gifford Lectures last year - "Silence in Christian History". It's a fascinating book not only because it's about contemplative silence, the silence that waits. It's about the ugly silence of the cover-up, the silence of things not admitted. He talks about the Church's silence on slavery. This is what he said about slavery in this book:

"The distressing fact for modern Christians is that slavery is taken for granted in the Bible, even if it's not considered to be a good thing at least for oneself. One would have to have been exceptionally independent minded and intellectually awkward to face up to the consensus of every philosopher in the ancient world and the first Christians did not rise to the challenge. Paul's epistle to Philemon in which the apostle asks his correspondent to allow him the continued services of Philemon's slave, Onesimus, is a Christian foundation document in the justification of slavery. It took us 1800 years to get rid of it."

What I didn't know is that the first Christians who challenged it, according to McCulloch, were the Pennsylvanian Quakers of 1688. They were the first in the game to challenge this. Here's McCulloch again: "Quakers believed in the prime authority of the inner light. Many of their earliest activists had, through their sharp critique of the problems of the scriptural texts, pioneered the modern enlightenment discipline of biblical criticism. The Quakers' disrespect for the established convention of biblical authority was the reason they could take a fresh approach to biblical authority and reject it. It took original minds to kick against the authority of sacred scriptures. What was needed was a prior conviction in one's conscience of the wrongness of slavery, which one then might justify by a purposeful re-examination of the Bible."

Note those words: "What was needed was a prior conviction in one's conscience of the wrongness of slavery". In other words, the Quakers decided that slavery was wrong. We know that. If the Bible appears to justify slavery, then the Bible is wrong. They created, by that moral supremacist approach to scripture, the beginnings of the scientific critique of scripture that we all live and wrestle with.

But not completely! Because one of the problems that Christians have, because of our attachment to the theory of revelation, is that we find it almost impossible to do the right things for the right reason without a religious justification. We can't just decide that it's absurd not to ordain women and just to do it: we have to find religious reasons for doing it. I remember when we were debating it in the Scottish Church – and you had your own versions in England – we raided the scriptures for texts to allow us to ordain women and we found one of course. There's a wee verse in Galatians, remember it? "In Christ there is neither slave nor free, male nor female, Jew nor Greek". Thank God. We breathe a sigh of relief. We had a scriptural mandate for doing the right thing. Then we started doing it. Unfortunately Paul didn't add "neither gay nor straight", did he? Could we not now say, "Yes, we have learned the inappropriateness of the subordination of women, we know that it is wrong: we have our inner light, our conscience, which tells ourselves we have permission?

I feel affection towards the churches struggling with the ordination of women, struggling intensively about gay relationships. You have to respect people who have integrated within their hearts and minds, as it were, this idea of authority, that doesn't enable them to think something for the first time and move into a new understanding of truth and morality and justice because they are held with this pious approach to the tradition. I respect that. There's something quite moving and beautiful about it. There was a headline in a Scottish newspaper not very long ago. There was a woman standing outside a house in the Highlands. She had been running it as a bed and breakfast place and she refused to allow a couple of gay men to spend the night there and she got done for it so she was selling the business because she had broken the law – because there is a law that prevents that. There was a picture of her standing outside. My heart went out to her because I realised she was being faithful to her tradition. Her tradition had taught her to believe that what these men would have done in that bed was an abomination. A priest friend of mine left me in his will a Victorian plate of the sort that hangs above the bed in cold bedrooms in the Highlands. It's a big eye and beneath it says "Thou, God, sees me". So in a sense you have to respect the loyalty of people to the tradition and it makes even kind people cruel because they're being faithful.

Maybe one of the lessons we have to learn is a kind of loosening, a kind of lightening up of the understanding of our institutions and organisations, our sacred scriptures, our texts - things that help us understand and interpret and make our way through this muddled existence, but, if you hold them too tightly, you idolatrise them in fact. If you turn them into gods, then you make it impossible to change your mind, certainly quickly, even at all. It's the most faithful people that find it most difficult to make these changes. This is the thing that breaks my heart about the debates that we're having. Of course you've got the people who are secret haters and love to have a scriptural text that gives them permission to do the thing they deeply hatefully want to do - but that's not true of most people. Most people are simply imprisoned in the theory, a theory of revelation, a theory of permanence, and wouldn't it be wonderful if we could all liberate ourselves from this and say "It's so uncertain where all this stuff came from. It's full of beauty, truth, mercy and forgiveness." It's also full of ancient attitudes that we should give ourselves permission to pick our way through. One of the things that's most helped me in my wrestling and struggle with all of this is a theory of art that I discovered from a philosopher called Arthur Danto. Danto said of the human being: we are extraordinary creatures, we human beings. Our minds, our big brains, are wrestling with this kind of stuff. Whether left, right or middle, we are all at it because in us, our evolution has gifted us with an intelligence that's a curse and a blessing.

The cows in the field - if there are any cows in Derbyshire - are not doing what we are doing tonight because they're so embedded in nature they're not asking these questions, but we are, we are doing it all the time. Danto's term for the human animal was *ens representans*, a being representing the world. Now let's think about that. One of the things that's most characteristic of us is that we're embedded in this world. We represent it. We make paintings of it. We write stories about it. Samuel Beckett said of James Joyce that he didn't write about something. When you read James Joyce you get the thing itself. He represents reality. He's got that mystical, magical ability to get into language what is actually happening, that walk through Dublin in Ulysses. Great artists do this. That's why they make us pause. You read a great novel and it's representing you. If it's a picture, even if it's just cows in a field, a tumbledown bridge, you're stunned by it. We are the creatures that represent the world back to ourselves. It means that we're not simply material creatures. Danto was very sure about this. He said if you simply materialise the human animal, you miss it's most important function. This ability to represent, to create art, and religion is one of our greatest creations.

Religion is us representing our search, our struggle to understand, to find meaning, wrestling with the possibility there may not be meaning. We are thrust into a universe with a lust for meaning, a universe that may not have meaning. That's one of the paradoxes that keeps me on the edge of transcendence. I don't do God very well these days, but I find myself poised on this kind of cliff – this strange mystery that I am a being who asks questions of the universe. It's taken the universe 16 billion years, but in us it's asking questions about it. In us it's wrestling with the big questions of meaning. But we have this tendency to jump too soon to the permanent answers. It slows the whole thing down. You miss it's most important function. It says the bus has stopped and it's all been answered, but we know it hasn't. We know the answer so we go on representing the universe to ourselves constantly. I don't pray much nowadays, not in the way I used to. I find a leaden-ness in saying morning and evening prayer, which I did every day for forty years. I can't do that now. But on two occasions recently I was prompted to a kind of prayer that was poetry rather than prose. I can't do the prose of God but I can do the poesis of God, the making of God. The word poetry comes from the Greek word for making. I found myself visiting a former priest in the diocese of Edinburgh who's been fighting cancer for years. He's lost all his vocal chords, had his gullet removed and he can't speak. He speaks on an i-pad. He was immensely cheerful and we were sitting there gossiping about bishops and what a dismal lot they were. It was all extremely enjoyable. Before I left, I said I wanted to pray with him. I wanted to bless him. So I stood up, put my hands upon his head and I made poetry over him. I blessed him in the name of the Three. I don't believe in the Trinity as a dogma or doctrine, but I was pouring the power, the grace and the strength of the Three into that man. I was making something happen. It was a work of art. I couldn't have justified it theologically or philosophically, but it was true, it meant something in that situation.

A few weeks later, at the end of High Mass in Old St Paul's where I still attend, I saw a clergyman in the congregation whom I didn't recognise. I saw a black suit. Ah, an Anglo-Catholic. I recognised the brand. Just as I was going downstairs for coffee, he came towards me with a man. He said he was a priest in a diocese in England and his bishop had given him permission to have a civil partnership with this man, but just a civil partnership. He couldn't do any more. Would I bless them? Would I give them a nuptial blessing? I took them into the Lady Chapel and I put my hands on them and I gave them a radical Trinitarian blessing, bonding them together. Tears were pouring down their faces. They didn't believe what I was doing. I was making God present, as it were, as an act of poetry. I was representing to them and to myself a longing for their unity for the struggle there had been, for the hurt that they felt, for a church that they'd worked for, that had somehow rejected them.

So I can't argue any of this. I'm lured into these situations where the *ens representans*, the being that represents, the being that pours its longings into acting, poetry and music and beauty, somehow makes that mystery present. Very fleetingly of course. I can't make a theory out of it. It's one of the problems that we're all wrestling with – at least some of us are wrestling with - that the God we meet in the theory doesn't do that, doesn't break down and creep up on people and offer them what you often get hints of. There are more than hints of it in Jesus – that insane, absolute unconditional grace, forgiveness and total acceptance of us and brokenness and loss and there's no way of being worthy of that. You get all that, all the hints of that in this God thing we're all wrestling with. I've ceased to be able to talk about God and to argue for God. I get lots of people trying to bring me back to God. I get one book a week from someone who says "This will sort you. This will really . . . ". As if I'd never gone through any of that stuff. I even get texts from the Bible – as if I'd never read it. I get all that kind of stuff. What I'm saying here is that there's something going on in our culture. This is seeing religion as somehow no longer opening the way to this poesis, this poetry of the possibility of ultimate meaning, but somehow shutting the door on it because it says it's all been answered, it's all back there.

Two people who've also helped me hold on to a strange Zen-way of doing this are two great Jews: Paul Celan, the poet, who committed suicide like Levy. He wrote an astonishing poem called "Psalm", in which the human being the *ens representans*, is praising nothingness because, if it's nothingness from which we come, out of that nothingness has come beauty and grace and forgiveness and horror and terror and ugliness. He praised nothingness. Here is the poem.

Psalm

No-man kneads us again out of Earth and Loam,
no-man spirits our Dust.
No-man.

Praise to you, No-man.
For love of you
we will flower.
Moving
towards you.

A Nothing
we were, we are, we shall
be still, flowering:
the Nothing-, the
No-man's-rose.

With
our Pistil soul-bright,
our Stamen heaven-torn,
our Corolla red
with the Violet-Word that we sang
over, O over
the thorn.

The thorn is the need to find meaning, to find beauty in an apparently meaningless universe. 'A Nothing' ('Ein Nichts' in the original language) came from nothing and we are the being that represents that back to itself. We don't know whether we're hearing an echo of that. I can live without it now. I can live with the possibility of what I try to represent we say back to the world, representing it, painting it, making it. It is enough. All the quarrels that are going on between the ultra-godly and the ultra-godless leave me cold, I'm afraid. I find myself in no-man's land, in Arnold's darkening plain where these armies battle by night. I'm not even very keen on attempts to revive the church's ability to communicate meaning because somehow I just want the church to shut up for a bit. I want a period of Sabbath. For myself I'm sick and tired of my own voice frankly. I'm taking a vow of silence next year for that reason. For I've being doing so much of talking, we're all chattering - E M Forster's 'poor little talkative Christianity'. Somehow these acts of poetry sometimes happen, these blessings, these moments of grace. They hold us in a strange kind of posture of waiting. R S Thomas said the meaning is in the waiting; don't jump too quickly to a conclusion. Wait, wait.

My other Jew is George Steiner. Amazing man. He's a very ill man now. In his little memoir, "Errata", he says something that you won't understand. Don't try to understand it: try to get the Zen of it. Let it kind of filter through and maybe it will alter the way in which you represent being. He says from the unreasoned unanalysable, often ruinous, all power of love stems the thought that God is not yet. That he will come into being, or more precisely, into manifest reach of human perception only when there is an immense success of love over hatred. Each and every cruelty, each and every injustice inflicted on man or beast justified the findings of atheism in so much as it prevents God from coming. But I am unable even at the worst hours to abdicate from the belief that the two validating wonders of mortal existence are love and the invention of the future tense. Their conjunction, if it will ever come to pass, is the Messianic. When love and the future tense marry, conjunct together, will be the Messianic.

I don't know what it means. Don't do the meaning thing. Don't turn it into a system – just live with the Zen and the impossibility of it. Love and the future tense in conjunction and remember that we humans are the beings that represent the world to itself. My wee dog doesn't do it. The cows and the sheep in the field don't. We uniquely do it: it is our pain, our passion and our glory. One of the things we've invented to do it is religion. See it as a work of art, therefore, as something we've created to represent mystery and the possibility that there may be meaning in a universe that scarily might not have meaning. We know this planet is going to die the heat death. All will be long gone. Some of us will soon be gone. I know I haven't got long. It will become a little cinder. I sometimes meditate on the fact that in that cinder's history there has been Bach, Mozart and Canterbury Cathedral, Tolstoy's "War and Peace", and innumerable acts of mercy and love and pity. Music cascading and all the horrors and it will be as if it had never been. What will it have all meant? The being that represented something and then shrivelled into a cinder? I don't know. But it will have been what it will have been - something glorious, something extraordinary will have happened through us in this burnt-out universe. That kind of makes it worthwhile because we, the being that represents the world back to itself will have imagined and longed for these glories and, even if they ultimately never existed, it will have been enough to have been gloriously wrong and sordidly right.

Questions and Discussion Starters

1. In what ways has God and the church been edited/revised/abandoned in your experience?

2. Should Christians find a religious justification for doing what is 'right'? Are we imprisoned in a theory of revelation?

3. What do you think of the idea that religion is 'us representing our search for meaning to the world'?

4. How capable are we of understanding and loving those with whom we profoundly disagree but who are being faithful to their tradition?

5. 'Don't try to understand it: try to get the Zen of it.' What about this approach to religion?

6. How do you respond to Paul Celan's poem?

7. Would you value a 'Sabbath' from 'poor little talkative Christianity'?

Notes:

Notes:

Notes: